THE JOB HUNTER'S WORKBOOK

THE JOB HUNTER'S WORKBOOK

Judith Taggart
Lynn Moore
Mary Naylor

Peterson's Guides
Princeton, New Jersey

Copyright © 1989 by Peterson's Guides, Inc.

Previous editions copyright © 1987, 1986, 1985 by JT&A, Inc.

All rights reserved. No part of this book may be reproduced, stored in a retrieval system, or transmitted, in any form or by any means—electronic, mechanical, photocopying, recording, or otherwise—except for citations of data for scholarly or reference purposes with full acknowledgment of title, edition, and publisher and written notification to Peterson's Guides prior to such use.

ISBN 0-87866-800-4

Composition and design by Peterson's Guides

Illustrations by David Merrill

Printed in the United States of America

10 9 8 7 6 5 4 3 2 1

CONTENTS

Foreword vii

Introduction ix

Career Connector xi

1   **If the Shoe Fits** 1
    ... exercises to help you "take your measure"

2   **Looking for a Home** 9
    ... in general, where and what kind of places are right for you

3   **You've Got What It Takes** 35
    ... assessing your skills

4   **You Know Somebody Who Knows Somebody** 53
    ... finding out where the jobs really are

5   **Would Your Own Mother Recognize You?** 67
    ... resumes, cover letters, etc.

6   **Dracula Will See You Now** 87
    ... the interview and the questions asked

7   **But Our President Doesn't Make That Much!** 101
    ... salaries, benefits, and perquisites

FOREWORD

What do you want to do with your life? Or rather, what *should* you do with your life—that's really the question.

And the answer lies within these pages. Not that it's the same answer for every reader—this workbook is the ultimate puzzle. As you carefully fit the pieces together (the pieces you alone design), the real you emerges. The real you at any age, any stage of life.

Originally written for use in career seminars for college students, the workbook solves career problems for others as well—the career changer, the retiree looking for new challenges, the junior high student groping for a fix on life.

Elusive though the solution may seem, you're never too old—or too young—to ponder what you should be doing with the rest of your life. A puzzle it is, indeed, but you alone can configure its pieces. Enjoy putting it together, and discovering your own answer, as you use this workbook.

INTRODUCTION

Almost no one enjoys job hunting. It's very stressful. The exercises in this book will help you to keep stress under control, make the most of your assets, and land a job that suits your abilities and needs.

Most job hunters worry about whether they'll find a job at all and ignore how much that job is going to mean to them later on. Yet they will spend more waking time with the job they take than with any person.

The job you take will:

1. Determine what time you get up in the morning.

2. Make you dress to please it five or six days a week.

3. Give you a fair allowance or keep you too poor to do anything you want.

4. Influence your health and, what's more, determine how much medical care you can afford.

5. Tell the whole world what kind of person you are just by what you do.

6. Let you know if it's okay to go off on a long weekend.

7. Influence how many people you see every day, how much time you spend with them, and what you're allowed to say to them.

Things like that make people run away from home, scare them away from marriage. But people take jobs readily, without ever worrying about life after the honeymoon.

This book is about not only how to find and get a job but how to land one you'd like to live with. Here's the first thing you should know: there is no such thing as a dead-end job. In theory, the guy who rides on the back of the trash truck can watch what's going on, buy himself a couple of trucks some day, outmarket the competition, turn a better profit with creative management, and end up living in a million-dollar home on the water. In some businesses the president used to be the secretary!

So does that mean anything will do for you? No. Negative factors do exist. Some you can control, and some you can't. Starting today, you should look at potential jobs in a new way: decide to take charge of what's controllable and to recognize what isn't. If you don't like the uncontrollables and think you can never accept them, then keep looking. None of the pluses will seem good enough later on.

> **There is no such thing as a dead-end job.**

Even though there are no dead-end jobs, dead ends do happen. There are three main reasons why:

1. The person doesn't match the opportunity at hand.
2. The person causes the dead end by his or her own attitude or habits.
3. The company doesn't like its own employees.

The first two reasons are under your control, usually. The last isn't. This book will begin by looking at *you*. Put career in the background for now. Your career will come out of thinking correctly about the job you're looking for. A career isn't anything more than making the most of yourself in the context of work. First you have to land the kind of job that will make that possible. But even before that, you have to get a realistic picture of your own personality and skills.

This book gives you a job-rating system that covers the information you need to get a good job and build a career.

Career Connector

HOBBIES

1.

2.

3.

SCHOOL SUBJECTS

1.

2.

3.

VOLUNTEER/WORK EXPERIENCE

1.

2.

3.

GEOGRAPHICAL PREFERENCES

1.

2.

3.

COMPANY TYPES

1.

2.

3.

INTERESTS

1.

2.

3.

OTHERS' PERCEPTIONS

1.

2.

3.

JOB MOTIVATORS/ENHANCERS

1.

2.

3.

CAREER/PERSONAL BALANCE

_____

_____

_____

SALARY RANGE

_____   _____

(low)   (high)

Once you have completed the Career Connector, you need to formulate a career objective. This is done by weaving all of the elements of your Career Connector together.

Career Objective

Example:

> *I would like to use my writing ability, editorial experience, ability to research, creativity, and concern for the environment, working as a writer/editor for a publication produced by a national organization with offices in Boston. I want to be in a position where I can influence others and to have a great deal of responsibility and autonomy. I want to make $26,000 a year and work no more than 55 hours a week, leaving time to go to the gym three times a week, attend a play once a month, and socialize with friends.*

As you can see, this objective is much more specific than "I want to work with people" or "I want to work in public relations." You want your career objective to be specific enough to give you a definite direction; however, not so specific that it eliminates potential options.

CAREER OBJECTIVE

_____
_____
_____
_____
_____
_____
_____
_____
_____
_____
_____
_____
_____
_____
_____
_____
_____

Chapter 1

IF THE SHOE FITS

The original job-hunting tactic was to go out and stand in a line. Usually the wrong one. The hundreds of men who couldn't pull Arthur's sword from the stone and women who couldn't get their big toe in Cinderella's slipper were fairly typical job hunters. Of course, professionals don't actually stand in line anymore; they just add their resume to the stack or make appointments. Although they don't see the other job hunters, it's still a line. And like the would-be Cinderellas and Arthurs, most of us insist on standing in the wrong one.

The Arthur and Cinderella stories exaggerate a basic truth of job hunting: you can't wear Cinderella's slipper and you can't handle Arthur's sword. But don't overlook the obvious. There are swords and slippers in other sizes too, including yours.

Before you start your job hunt, take your measure. Your best chance is in the job that really fits you. In a world full of talented people, it's easy to feel a little unprepared, a bit second-rate. Even people who usually feel okay begin to wonder about themselves after a few dismal weeks of job hunting.

The job interview—that's the one thing you want out of all your efforts. Your prospective employers want someone to fit into their needs and organization. Save yourself some trouble. Use as much good sense as you would if you were shoe shopping. You wouldn't jam your foot into every sample shoe that looked good. You'd limit your trying on to the shoes that were reasonably likely to feel good. Job-shop only for what fits you.

Whether you fit the job depends on two key points:

1. How many of the employer's wants can you fulfill?
2. How rigidly are the employer's needs defined?

Before you can tackle either question, you must know yourself very well. This is a must. You probably won't ever walk into an employer's office and be told you're perfect (honestly, anyway). You will get clues about what the employer values, however. Pounce on them.

When you hear of something that sounds like you—you must be ready to prove you have the qualifications for it. When the match is not perfect, you'll have to show that what you do have will work.

Finding Yourself—The Short Course

To begin with, this book will show you how to assess your job personality. You've heard of people who drop out of normal life to "find themselves." Well, that's a little extreme. The exercises presented here will help you to figure out pretty quickly what kind of a working person you are.

You should do the exercises in the order you come to them in the text, but it is important to finish them in two weeks, maximum. You could spend a lifetime exploring the questions they pose, but if you don't get through them quickly, you will lose the connections and not reap the full benefit from them.

> **Get interviews for jobs you are likely to fit.**

To help you keep track of time, fill in the starting and finishing dates on each exercise. Some people procrastinate or habitually start more than they can finish. If you are one of those, use a calendar you see every day to check your progress, and tell a couple of people you are sure will keep asking about your progress, what you are doing.

If you have been long unemployed, laid off, or fired, you may have difficulty doing these exercises. But they are even more important for you. It is hard to face the world when you aren't feeling particularly good about yourself. These exercises will help you sort out things and find your real identity. Identity is the point of these exercises—you do still have one! You may also uncover some surprising mismatches between the place where you used to work and the kind of place that would be good for the real you.

The Career Connector

The gray sheet at the beginning of this chapter is your Career Connector. As you complete the exercises and read the chapters, you should jot down what you learn on the Career Connector.

Suggestions for where to do this are given several times through the text, but don't be limited by that. You should write anything you find useful in it.

Once you have completely filled in the Career Connector, you should develop a career objective that sums up what you have learned about who you are and where you want to go. Take the ideas from the Career Connector, resolve any conflicts among them, and compose the rest into a clear pattern pointing to a valid career objective. This is for your use only, not for a resume. Consider it your "hidden agenda" and tell the bold truth. If you are exploring several options at this point, write as many career objectives as you need to cover the territory.

The Career Connector may not look very sophisticated, but it is very important. Make a photocopy of it to keep with you as you respond to job openings, look up job information, or write a resume.

Exercise 1
You're Terrific!

Write down one accomplishment that you feel particularly good about. Pick something you are truly proud of.

_____
_____
_____
_____
_____
_____
_____
_____

Review this achievement and list the skills and personality traits it took to accomplish it. Ask your friends or family what skills they think you used.

Your list: **Others' perceptions:**

_____   _____
_____   _____
_____   _____
_____   _____
_____   _____
_____   _____
_____   _____

When you finish this exercise, take time to notice and enjoy the feeling of optimism that comes from focusing on your assets.

Exercise 2
Your Interests

Some counselors suggest an autobiographical approach to investigating who you are. We are going to keep it more informal and more fun to do. The object here is to find your lifelong interests.

1. Get a poster-sized piece of blank paper; tear open a grocery bag if need be.

2. Beginning with childhood, write down every hobby you ever had—including those you no longer pursue. Write your favorites (at the time you did them) in very large letters. Put the earliest ones toward the top, the most recent at the bottom.

3. Now write down all your burning interests—this includes anything you have ever read several books about and things you've always wanted to try but never gotten around to.

4. Write down all the school subjects you did well in. If you made A's in everything, write down only your personal favorites.

5. Write down everything people have told you you did well, even if you don't quite see it.

6. Of the volunteer and paid work experiences you have had, list the particular things you did well—consider both specific tasks and general abilities.

7. Stand back and take a look at all this. What kinds of related activities appear? Write down a key word or phrase that sums the one that appears most often, for example, language ability, dealing with people, fixing things, organizing. If you need help thinking of a key word, see the clue list of functional skills at the end of this exercise.

Treasurer - best records! Wrote a radio ad.
Set up club library.   *Coached little league.*
Illustrated the "lake" booklet. *Created volunteer*
Straightened out membership records. *"fair share" system.*
                                    Took inventory (Jake's).
                                    ADMINISTRATION

8. Draw a circle around your key word in a colored pen. Circle everything that goes with it in the same color and draw a line connecting them with the key word.

(Treasurer - best records!) Wrote a radio ad.
(Set up club library.)   *Coached little league.*
Illustrated the "lake" booklet. *(Created volunteer*
(Straightened out membership records.) *"fair share" system.)*
                                    Took inventory (Jake's).
                                    (ADMINISTRATION)

Hobbies

- (Reading)
- Archery + rifle (target)
- Camping
- Canoeing
- Sewing, designing, knitting
- Furniture refinishing
- Woodworking
- Cooking and eating
- (Writing)

Subjects

- (English)
- Geometry (the only math I really liked!)
- Zoology
- (All language and literature classes)
- Anthropology
- Art (jr. high)
- Art (college — sculpture)
- (All writing assignments)

Well-dones

- Various wood projects
- (Writing — from elem. school to college, + still — always encouraged to pursue)
- Sewing
- Cooking (but I don't want to cook for a living!)
- Training others
- (Speaking (avoid this, but others liked it))
- Brochures, etc.

Interests

- (Sign languages)
- Archaeology
- (Musicology — English to Appalachia oral tradition
- Writing — devt. of symbols to alphabet
- Grammar — theories, esp. transformations)
- Sailing
- Trees — wood types + uses
- Medicine — genetics
- Sculpture
- Photography
- Colors — uses + psychology
- Art — apprec. + history

Volunteer/Work

- Bookstore (1st job, from ordering to banking at 16)
- Nurse's Aide — liked writing charts + administering treatments best
- (Writing newspaper ads)
- Creating special displays
- Training new employees
- Helping others get promotions
- (Counseling teens)
- Purchasing — redid system
- Designing books, brochures, etc.
- Financial planning + projections
- (Rewriting (heavy editing))
- Proposals

SKILLS — KEY WORDS

- Language ability
- Persuasion — in writing
- Artistic — perception

9. Look again for another prominent activity. Use another color for your key word and circle and connect that group.

10. After looking at all this, select as many as three activities or traits from each group—hobbies, work, subjects, volunteer experience, "well-dones," and interests—that you would like to incorporate in your ideal job. Transfer your selections to the Career Connector. Use your own imagination and other resources to find a few occupations that would use your strongest interests, and if you are still uncertain what you want to do for a living, investigate these suggestions.

Key Word Clue List: Functional Skills

(Skills developed through education and training)

Researching	Constructing	Planning
Investigating	Conversing	Arranging
Analyzing	Advising	Organizing
Questioning	Counseling	Coordinating
Comparing	Listening	Delegating
Conceptualizing		Managing
Classifying		Attending to detail
Systematizing	Empathizing	Monitoring
Summarizing	Helping	Troubleshooting
Evaluating	Relating well to others	Initiating
Observing	Implementing	
Perceiving		
Reasoning		Deciding
Assessing	Presenting	Effecting change
Appraising	Public speaking	Expediting
Anticipating	Writing	Recommending
	Editing	
	Translating	
Promoting	Reporting	Accounting
Proposing	Interpreting	Calculating
Persuading	Teaching	Computing
Influencing	Coaching	Budgeting
Politicking	Training	Measuring
Motivating	Leading discussions	Keeping records
Mediating	Explaining	Problem solving
Designing	Performing	Operating
Drawing	Entertaining	Repairing

Chapter 2

LOOKING FOR A HOME

In the last chapter you started to learn something about yourself. Now, where do you want to work? The better you know yourself, the better you can answer the question. Have you already decided that IBM is the answer—or anywhere in Fort Lauderdale? Pay attention anyway. "Where do you want to work?" asks more than that.

The right place must meet several needs—your needs. Finding it is a very personal process. You must pick the best answer, given what you know, what matters most to you, and what you can tolerate.

Look at the things you must consider:

1. Geography

Obviously "where" includes where on the map. The less this matters to you, the more likely you'll be able to meet your other needs. If you're really itching to go to the opposite coast or halfway around the world, however, do some research. The person who grew up bullying his or her way through New York City will have to readjust mightily to get along with the natives in Des Moines. Sunny Florida may sound wonderful; does living in a retirement community sound as good? Before you jump, check the surroundings. If you can't visit, then find people who know the area and ask them what it's really like.

The opposite side of this question concerns staying put. Are you really tied down where you are, or just inventing excuses? In most cases, you'd be better off to be somewhat open to the idea of relocation. If not now, a later promotion could depend on your willingness to move.

Select three preferred geographic locations and add them to the Career Connector.

2. Autonomy

Some people would rather risk failure than follow the tried and true. One of the worst possible errors is to put yourself in an environment totally the opposite of your personality.

Companies run the entire gamut from the absolute authority structure of the military to the freewheeling individualism of an artists' cooperative. In addition to whether you fit the atmosphere right now, you should consider if you'll still fit a few years and promotions later.

Ask yourself these key questions:

1. Do I tolerate, welcome, or hate close supervision?

2. Do I feel comfortable making decisions on my own?

3. Do I mind taking risks?

4. Would I rather be told what to do clearly or told to fix a problem however I can?

5. Do I enjoy managing or supervising others?

6. Can I tell other people that they are not doing well in a way that improves their performance?

7. Would I rather work alone, on a team, or with some of both?

8. Do I like routine? Do I dislike it so much I'd end up hating my job?

You have the idea. Be sure you use your interviews to find out how your prospective organization fits your performance.

3. Recognition

Everyone needs to be recognized, but how much and in what way do you need it? Despite good pay for the skill level and superb benefits, most people hate assembly-line jobs. It is not the physical conditions that become unbearable, it is the dehumanizing character of the job.

All organizations recognize employees in some manner but the styles vary widely. At one extreme are companies whose executives are golden and everyone else is expendable. Even being an executive in such a place can be unpleasant for people who identify closely with those working under them. Others will enjoy the distinction.

Some companies work so hard to create "one big happy family" that everyone is rewarded—for having a birthday or a baby, passing a course, sticking around, you name it. People who want a strong overlap between social life and work life enjoy this hometowniness. Others find it annoying and prefer only job-related recognition.

4. Opportunity

Most jobs present avenues for growth. But you will have to decide whether you'd rather grow within one company or transfer your skills up and out. Companies that prefer to hire managers from the outside offer little upward mobility for lower or entry-level employees. This is not necessarily bad. If you are cultivating a high-demand skill, you could benefit from the training. But you would have to sell your improved skills elsewhere to be fairly rewarded. It is important to ask the hiring interviewer what the opportunities for advancement are.

> **Good salaries pale without challenging work.**

It is just as important to know the field at large. If the company is a recognized leader, little advancement within it is not instant death. In overcrowded fields, the average or even above-average person will need to break in wherever possible.

Another aspect of opportunity is company growth. A small company will have fewer spots to fill as you get ready for advancement, but if it is growth oriented and you contribute all along, you can move very fast. Even companies with many high-level jobs may not have many openings in them.

In addition to opportunity for advancement, you should consider opportunity to work. Does a paycheck amply reward you, or do you place great value on doing "meaningful" work? A good salary can grow pale in attraction if the level of challenge does not keep pace.

The kinds of opportunity you should investigate include:

1. Advancement
2. Skill development
3. Increasing responsibility
4. Training

5. Company Size

Working for a small, new company is very different from working for a large, established company. On the average, larger companies can afford to pay entry-level employees better and provide grander benefit packages. Smaller companies can tax your drive and creativity to their fullest, however, since they need every employee's maximum contribution to survive. What do you want? For every generality exceptions exist. The small company can be ruled by a despot who will squelch every idea you present. Some large companies make a special effort to keep a small-company "feel."

In general, the choice between small or large comes down to these issues:

Small Company	Large Company
Lower starting pay but may match larger companies at higher levels	Higher starting pay often remaining higher
Few benefits; chance for responsibility can be high from start	Greater benefit packages; responsibility usually earned more slowly
Chance to influence management and policy at lower levels except where owner/board, etc., prefers high control	Influence management and policy at higher levels except by suggestion or other formal routes or unusual initiative
High personal recognition; informal demonstration procedures	Low personal recognition; formalized procedures
Promotion opportunity limited by company size and fortunes	Promotion opportunity limited by policy and turnover; more slowly affected by minor changes in company fortunes
Training on the job; can be extended to other jobs and departments more readily	Outside training more likely to be permitted or encouraged

Not one of these comparisons is absolutely true. Decide which approach you prefer and see what the company you are considering does.

But remember, companies with fewer than 100 employees will generate 80 percent of new jobs.

Which Companies Are Best?

Depending on what you look for, several investigators have compiled lists of best companies to work for. Here are a few.

Fortune magazine surveys senior executives, directors, and financial analysts each year to pick America's 250 most admired companies (ten leaders in twenty-five different fields). The ratings are based on:

1. Quality of management
2. Quality of products and services
3. Innovativeness
4. Financial soundness
5. Ability to attract, develop, and keep talented people
6. Community and environmental responsibility
7. Use of corporate assets

Overall, the ten most admired companies in a recent survey were:

    Merck   Exxon
    Rubbermaid   PepsiCo
    3M   Boeing

Philip Morris   Herman Miller
Wal-Mart Stores   Shell Oil

Other researchers draw the list differently. Robert Levering, Milton Moskowitz, and Michael Katz reject profits, growth, and contented stockholders as earmarks of good employers. They emphasize good employer-employee relationships. To rate firms specifically, they choose pay, benefits, job security, advancement opportunity, and ambience. Here are their top ten:

Bell Labs   Hewlett-Packard
Trammell Crow   IBM
Delta Airlines   Pitney Bowes
Goldman Sachs   Northwestern Mutual Life
Hallmark Cards   Time, Inc.

These five more nearly made the list:

Advanced Micro Devices   3M
Merck   Publix Super Markets
J. P. Morgan

For women, the list changes a bit. Here Levering, Moskowitz, and Katz include these thirteen leaders:

Citicorp   Mary Kay Cosmetics
Control Data   Nordstrom
Doyle Dane Bernbach Northwestern Mutual Life
General Mills   J. C. Penney
Hallmark Cards   Security Pacific Bank
IBM   Time, Inc.
Levi Strauss

Mother Jones magazine looked at employment opportunity and financial rewards to choose these for women:

Campbell Soup Co.   Publix Super Markets
Hallmark Cards   North American Tool and Die
Dora Corp.   Kollmongen Corp.
W. L. Gore and Associates   Levi Strauss

For blacks, Levering, Moskowitz, and Katz praise the track records of these eight companies:

Cummins Engine   Levi Strauss
General Electric   Los Angeles Dodgers
Hewlett-Packard   Polaroid
IBM   Time, Inc.

What about working around family obligations? *Money* magazine found these employers tops:

Control Data   Procter and Gamble
Hewlett-Packard   Steelcase, Inc.
IBM   Stride Rite
Merck   3M
State of New York   U.S. Navy

Forbes magazine, with emphasis on profitability, chose a completely different top-ten list:

IBM	American Tel & Tel
Exxon	Philip Morris
Ford Motors	E. I. duPont
General Motors	BellSouth
General Electric	Sears, Roebuck

Finally, Thomas J. Peters, in his book *In Search of Excellence,* and in an interview published in *Inc.* magazine, cites the following companies as leaders:

Hewlett-Packard	Marriott Corp.
Emerson Electric	Dayton Hudson
Dora Corp.	Raychem Corp.
W. L. Gore and Associates	Walt Disney Products
3M	RMI
Procter and Gamble	Wal-Mart Stores
DuPont	McDonald's
Johnson and Johnson	Texas Instruments
Milliken	Frito-Lay
PepsiCo	J. C. Penney
Lockheed	

What Makes Them Good?

You may not find a job with any company on these lists. Competition is keen. So how do you spot a good employer?

The key is to remember you will be an *employee.* For your purposes, how they treat employees is much more telling than how they do in other areas.

Profitability matters when it concerns your job security, your stock options or profit-sharing plan, your bonuses, and so on.

Product quality matters to the extent it affects your pride and opportunity. If you intend to sell insurance, for example, you won't do well with a company that has too few products and too poor a choice of plans or with one that has a poor rating in the industry. But as Avis proved, you don't have to be No. 1 to crow.

What Do You Look for Then?

1. Management

Management style is probably the single most significant influence on how you enjoy your job from day to day. Bosses should not domineer but lead and encourage performance. And there should not be too many bosses. A world of difference exists between companies that select team leaders from the employees producing the genuine product and those that lump all producers into a subcategory to be watched cautiously by nonproducing managers. Top-level staff should be lean.

Control should be simple and straightforward. Complex systems for employee watching signify a suspicious nature—the management doesn't believe in its troops. Look out for companies with too many rules, procedures, standards, goals, policies, and so on.

An important question is whether you can reach the people that affect your job. Do you have to go through channels for every small concern, or can you work directly with your counterparts in other departments to resolve minor problems? Can you suggest improvements and adjustments or make complaints easily and effectively?

How do you find out about the management? Ask the people who work there.

2. Innovation

Yours and theirs. Companies that adjust to outside needs constantly create new products and services and are exciting to work for. Their good ideas come from employees—meaning that you will get a chance to prove your good ideas.

3. People Orientation

Some companies exist mainly for profit or some other goal. For them employees are a necessary evil. Other companies find employees the source and backbone of their success. You want the second kind.

4. Quality

Companies that provide excellent products and services, treating customers well, usually extend this concern to employees. Besides, most employees enjoy treating customers well.

5. Encouragement

Formal and informal chances to make the most of yourself will enhance your job. This includes allowing you to plan your own work, solve problems creatively, try new and risky ideas you believe in, and do things you haven't done before. Chances for training, education, and formal learning programs are also a big plus.

6. Compensation

You need the paycheck. It should be fair. A good benefit package often indicates a forward-looking company. But make sure options, bonuses, etc., don't influence you too much. You have to live. Also beware of companies that trade glamour for your sweat. Be very sure it's what you want before you decide the low beginning pay is worth it. Many industries thrive on eager, underpaid laborers knowing full well that most will not rise to the top where the money is.

7. Security

Security is a tricky thing to assess. Some of the most secure jobs are in places ambitious people don't want to work. Some of the highest paying are where the risk of losing the job is also high. Decide what you need in the way of security. If security depends upon performance and you think you can perform, the job may be quite safe for you (but not necessarily for someone else). No one, however, needs capriciousness. Ask about turnover. Were people fired because the owner habitually does that in a tantrum? That's a bad sign, no matter how competent you are.

For a good list of companies and discussion, read *The 100 Best Companies to Work for in America* by Levering, Moskowitz, and Katz (Addison-Wesley, 1984).

Company Types

In Chapter 1 you confronted a great many considerations that bear on finding a job that suits your personality. Now here is another list of things you should consider. Companies that fall into these categories will have a characteristic feel about them that may matter to you. For instance, where unionization is the rule, advancement by seniority rather than pure merit is likely to tag along. If you enjoy influencing public policy, the rules will be different in a nonprofit or educational organization from those in the profit-making sector. Think about these company characteristics and how they might influence your job.

    Manufacturing
    Service orientation
    Branch or franchise
    Local ownership
    National ownership
    Rigid hierarchy
    Loose hierarchy
    Size of organization
    Public sector
    Private sector
    Educational sector
    Nonprofit sector
    Union
    Nonunion
    Outdoors
    Indoors
    Physical environment
    Nature of work schedule

Select the three company traits that are most important to you. Transfer your selections to the Career Connector.

Where?

This still doesn't answer where you want to work, does it? But you do have an idea what the company should be like. The next chapter deals with job-hunting research. Research will lead you to the answer. You might not end up in one of the "100 best" companies, but you can find out if the companies you uncover are just as good.

Exercise 3
How You Handle Authority

This exercise is a chance for you to think about how you deal with authority—wielding your own and bending to others'. What is your reaction to these scenarios?

1. The person working next to you is overloaded. Your boss tells you to finish one of her jobs.

    a. You do it automatically.

    b. You feel a little pressure but do it willingly.

    c. You quickly review your own obligations and tell the boss whether you can do it.

    d. You point out that it isn't your responsibility but do it grudgingly.

    e. You refuse to do it on general principles.

2. A very good customer asks you to modify a standard service to fit his needs better.

    a. You explain that that is not an option.

    b. You tell him you'll have to ask your boss first.

    c. You tell him you'll arrange it but will call if you have any problems. You then work out a reasonable solution and sell it to your company.

    d. You bend several rules and combine parts of different services because you think keeping his business is well worth it. The customer gets an arrangement pretty close to what he asked for.

    e. You decide what to do to meet the customer's needs and just do it on your own.

3. You have several trainees working for you in a new department. It is time to reorganize and assign specific duties, naming a couple of working leaders.

    a. You know what you want and make the choices yourself.

    b. You have an idea how it should sort out but run it by your superior for approval before you say anything to anyone in the department. You announce the choices a couple of days later.

    c. You tell your employees that the reorganization is coming and you already have an idea of who is best at what. You tell them that you are open to suggestions, if they wish to make them, and will make a decision within two weeks.

    d. You tell your employees that you will be reviewing their records and interviewing each of them in the next couple of weeks for the new positions. Meanwhile, you keep an eye on how they react.

    e. You take your personnel records to your boss and wait for his opinion before you do anything further.

4. You switched secretaries with another manager because the secretaries did not get along very well with their respective bosses. Both secretaries objected vehemently at being moved, nonetheless.

    a. You told them it was the best choice and they should try to get along in their new spots.

b. You pointed out that they were not doing well in the previous arrangement and that the only options were to switch back, if they thought they could improve their performance, or to live with the new one.

   c. You explained that you thought this would be a good idea and asked them to try the new arrangement for a month. You also pointed out that their performance had been below par, and that the final choice would be worked out to their satisfaction as long as it did not disrupt the entire office.

   d. You told them you would consider moving them into new positions when the next opening came up.

   e. You moved them back.

5. Company policy requires a procedure that you know is inefficient and outdated.

   a. You follow it and tell your friends your company is inefficient.

   b. You follow it but grumble to your boss every once in a while.

   c. You get some support from your peers, then present an alternative to your boss in a meeting, knowing you can count on some positive reactions.

   d. You plan a completely new approach and present it to your boss: if he or she disapproves, you pursue it higher up.

   e. You've been doing it your way all along.

6. You read a report in the company newsletter that says that the Office Efficiency Institute found that extending the lunch break to an hour and a quarter actually increases efficiency for several reasons.

   a. You find that interesting and mention it to a friend later when you get on the subject.

   b. You think it sounds reasonable, particularly since it isn't just one person's opinion.

   c. You wonder who the Office Efficiency Institute is.

   d. Some reasons are sound, but you question others, and since you don't know anything about the research methods, you don't buy it as is.

   e. You figure it for propaganda and dismiss it.

7. You have one employee who isn't doing anything all day while the rest of the office is going full steam.

   a. You fire him.

   b. You redistribute some tasks and increase his duties.

   c. You tell him he isn't sharing the load and find out whether there is a reason he doesn't pick up some slack. You then see to it that a solution is found.

   d. You wait until his regular review and give him a "meets standards" rating (you give everyone else "exceeds standards").

   e. You wish he'd go away but don't do anything until you get a chance to transfer him to another department.

8. You have ordered 200 notebooks with the company logo on them. When they come, the address line is missing.

   a. You accept them anyway.

   b. You accept them but complain.

- c. You accept them but insist on a price adjustment for the error.
- d. You return them for correction at the supplier's cost.
- e. You return them and refuse payment.

9. You've done business with one company for many years, and they have been very reliable, almost family. Now you need a special billing arrangement that fits your new computer system. The company says they can't do it.

    - a. You have all their bills recoded manually to fit your system.
    - b. You recode the bills but you write another letter formally requesting the change to someone you know is pretty good at getting things through channels.
    - c. You recode for now but insist that future business depends upon their ability to meet your needs within the next 90 days.
    - d. You place the regular projects with this company as you look for another supplier to take over all the work eventually.
    - e. You cancel all jobs not already in the works, including routine business you have done with this company for many years. You do not pay any bills until they get this problem straightened out.

10. Your company was sold to a new owner. This company requires a lot of detail you are not used to, such as recording all phone calls, filling out a daily status report for all activities, and taking coffee breaks at specified intervals.

    - a. You do it.
    - b. It takes some getting used to. You comply most of the time but sometimes have to go back and try to fill in the reports at the end of the week when you turn them in. Occasionally you grab an extra coffee break if no one's watching.
    - c. You agree to the need to control the phone bill but think less detail is needed on the status sheet. Wherever you have other records that sufficiently verify your progress, you summarize what you did on the status sheet.
    - d. You help yourself to an extra coffee break when you come in early or have worked especially hard or late. You miss a lot of phone calls and actively complain about the status sheet. You even propose a more efficient control system.
    - e. You start looking for another job. You don't need a mama to tell you how much coffee you can have and, after bringing the subject up with the new management unsuccessfully, you've had it. Your status sheets are only half filled out, and you don't even bother to record local calls.

Evaluation

Now what does this amount to? Look at your answers.

1. Recheck them. Were you absolutely honest or did you put down what you thought you should do? What may seem wrong here is not the question at hand. The question is, How do you feel about authority? You need to recognize the true you and find a company that thinks the same way.

2. Score your answers. Tally up for scenarios 1, 5, 6, 9, and 10:

	For example:
____ a's x 1 = ____	0 a's x 1 = 0
____ b's x 2 = ____	1 b x 2 = 2
____ c's x 3 = ____	1 c x 3 = 3
____ d's x 4 = ____	1 d x 4 = 4
____ e's x 5 = ____	2 e's x 5 = 10
Total for section = _____	Total = 19
Divided by 5 = _____ (T score)	÷ 5 = $3^4/_5$

Tally up for scenarios 2, 3, 4, 7, and 8:

	For example:
____ a's x 1 = ____	0 a's x 1 = 0
____ b's x 2 = ____	0 b's x 2 = 0
____ c's x 3 = ____	1 c x 3 = 3
____ d's x 4 = ____	3 d's x 4 = 12
____ e's x 5 = ____	1 e x 5 = 5
Total for section = _____	Total = 20
Divided by 5 = _____ (G score)	÷ 5 = 4

3. Interpret. Scenarios 1, 5, 6, 9, and 10 deal with your response to orders. A score of 1 is extreme obedience, 3 is the balanced position between following orders readily and bucking them. The 3 position thinks it through but lives up to general expectations. A 5 doesn't take orders well at all but will always go his or her own route. People who are strongly on this end of the scale might consider self-employment as a good option if the skills, daring, and financial resources are at hand. Your score for this section is your "T score."

Scenarios 2, 3, 4, 7, and 8 ask how comfortable you are with giving orders. The most independent, demanding (and possibly insensitive) types would get a score of 5 here. Once again, 3 is the position between strong command and wishy-washiness. A score of 1 indicates extreme discomfort, even inability, in making any demands on people—even those paid to do a specific task. A person on the lower side of this skill could most happily give orders in limited settings—backed up by policy, procedures, and bosses willing to validate the action. This section yields your "G score."

You have probably guessed that G is for "give" and T is for "take."

4. Put it in perspective. You have two scores. What do they indicate about you in the business world? To find out, let's put you on the map. Put an *X* on the T-line where your T score falls. Put another X on the G-line where your G score falls. Draw perpendicular lines through these points to where they intersect, as in the example below. The quadrant your lines intersect in represents your authority style. The closer the intersection is to the center 3, the more flexible you can be. The closer to the top, the more readily you follow orders; the closer to the bottom, the more you resist. As your point of intersection moves left, the more you dislike being responsible for managing others. As it moves right, the more you enjoy being the final authority.

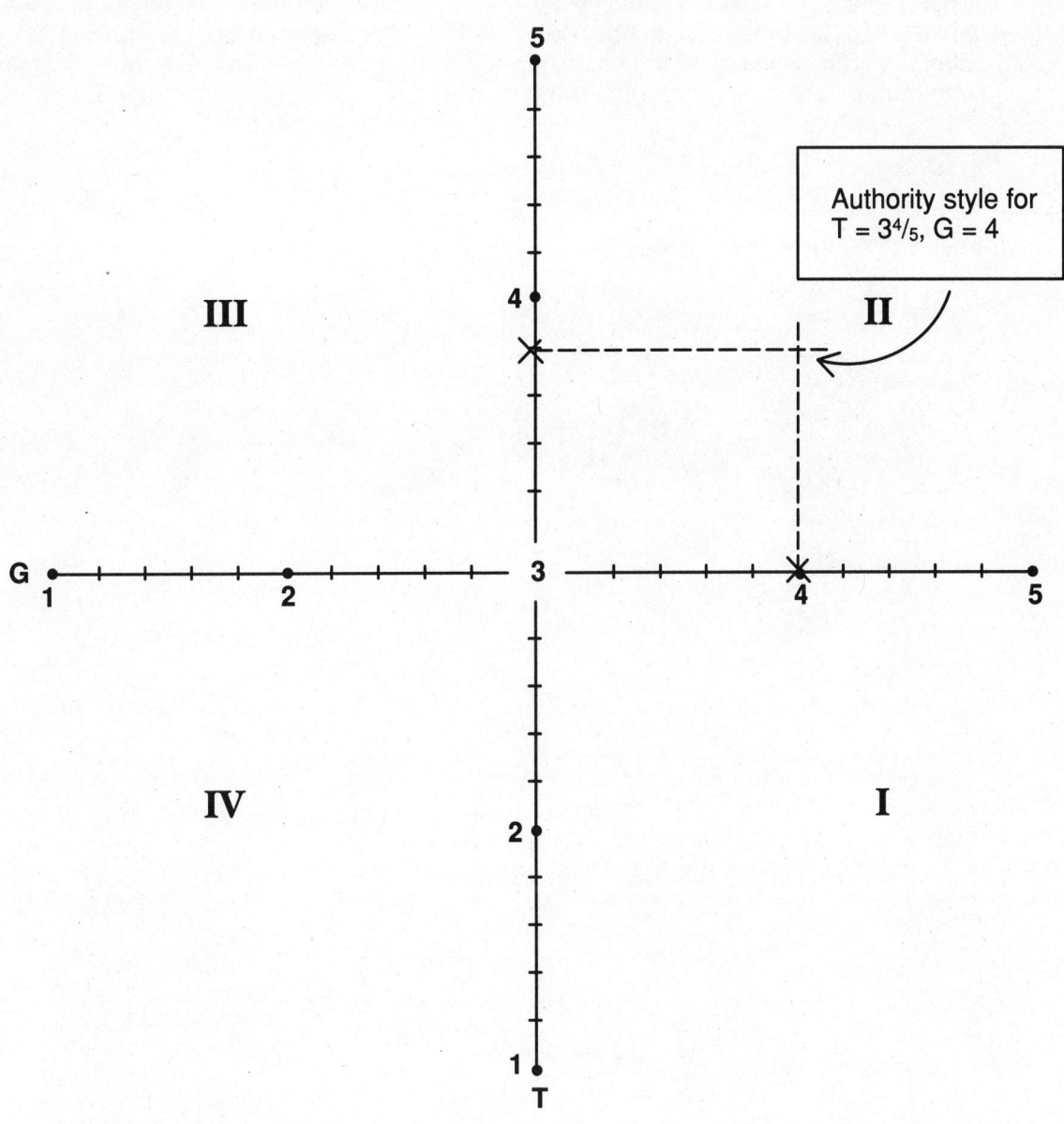

Which quadrant is your intersection in? Does one of the following descriptions seem to represent your organizational power approach?

I. The employee in this quadrant prefers to work uninterruptedly in her own manner, can organize or manage others, and is best in charge of a project alone or as a project leader. She can rise far if she doesn't get into trouble on the way up.

II. This person can work within strict guidelines, has the authority trait, can direct others, fits into a strong chain of command, and goes through channels.

III. Those in this quadrant should always work in a controlled situation where the rules and expectations are well known. They will also be okay in lower-level positions but are definitely not comfortable directing people. Management positions are doubtful unless they deal more with things or data than people.

IV. This person is a maverick, best left alone. He may produce valuable work but is likely to miss out unless cooperation is learned. He could originate ideas and plans and depend upon an aide to enforce them.

Exercise 4
Problem Solving

You have just inherited from your uncle a company that makes ceramic ovenware. The company is a mess. Its products are sturdy and useful but not widely known. The employees are fighting. Profits are falling every quarter. What would you do to turn this company around? To improve employee and employer morale?

Write your solutions before going any further. Give your imagination free rein.

Problem Solving

[blank lined box]

Your solutions can reveal a lot about your attitudes and what is important to you. Evaluate what they show about:

Dealing with people _____

Establishing goals _____

Creativity _____

Boldness or conservativeness _____

Handling of authority _____

Exercise 5
Job Satisfaction—What's Important?

What excites one person is very difficult for some others to tolerate. Think over the following list very carefully. Which considerations are most important to you in your job?

Motivators

_____ Autonomy

_____ Pay

_____ Challenging work

_____ Responsibility

_____ Clear guidance

_____ Security

_____ Being recognized

_____ Opportunity to grow

_____ Leisure time—I work to live

_____ Power or authority

Which one is absolutely your first consideration? Put a *1* by that choice. Continue to rank these choices, most important to least important (10th place).

Are you certain? Most people first wonder how much money they will get, but many people quit jobs despite good pay when they get tired of having somebody always overrule them or overlook them at promotion time or when the job just gets too boring. Change your ranking now if you wish to.

The job factors on this list are motivators. They are critical elements in employee satisfaction or dissatisfaction. Other factors that can affect a job might be called "enhancers." These may take on extreme importance to some people, or they may become important in special situations. Some of the enhancers could be included under your personal definition of a motivating factor; for instance, being recognized might include status. Other enhancers such as attractive surroundings or being ethical are so commonplace that they become important only when they are notably absent.

Put a check by the enhancer terms that matter most to you. Do any of these matter so much you would consider them a motivator? Where would you rank them among the other motivators?

Job Enhancers

_____ Location

_____ Variety

_____ Stimulation

_____ Status/prestige

_____ Travel

____ Being ethical/honest

____ Attractive surroundings

____ Other (specify) _____

  Select the three job motivators and enhancers that are most important to you. Transfer them to the Career Connector.

Exercise 6
What Makes You Happy?

This exercise consists of many pairs of almost identical jobs. The only differences between the two jobs in each pair are the features mentioned. Choose the job that you prefer in each pair.

A job with security (S)	One that pays much more but may end in two years (P)
A management position (C)	The same kind of work, but on your own (A)
One that offers excellent retirement benefits (S)	The other company seems to treat even lower-level employees with unusual respect and candor (R)
A chance to be in charge of a large department (R)	This one offers even more power—but it is behind the scenes (C)
Excellent pay (P)	Shorter hours (L)
Shorter hours and more vacation (L)	More variety and training (G)
Your name on the door of your office and on the company letterhead (R)	A chance to set up the department yourself and run it the way you think is best (A)
A vice presidency (R)	A chance to move up without working overtime (L)
Almost no supervision; you'll be totally busy every minute (A)	Less pressure but closer supervision (L)

$23,000 (P)	$20,000 and lots of contact with public figures as the company spokesman (R)
A management track for college grads (G)	A wider variety of duties to be learned quickly (M)
Fairly routine work with excellent pay and benefits (P)	More challenging work for which you are totally responsible, but slightly less pay (X)
You'll have to create profit by developing and marketing your own ideas (A)	A similar marketing situation with demanding quotas, but another department originates the products (X)
If you leave early, work will go undone (X)	With plenty of staff, you can use your leave whenever you like (L)
You know this organization is depending upon your skills to survive (X)	You won't make such a critical difference, and the company is on a sound financial basis (S)
You will have to approve all press releases before they go out (C)	You have enough else to do and will maintain responsibility, but an assistant does most of the reviews (R)
You have no big surprises most days even though the job is extremely important to the city government (X)	Everything is likely to go wrong anytime. You are the troubleshooter, because of your unique skills (M)
Your job is critical. Sometimes you have to go in on weekends or at night to keep up (X)	Your job is interesting and important, but not critical. Still, many people look to you for advice (R)
The turnover rate here is almost nil (S)	A more explosive environment, but you will manage a much larger department (C)
You will be expected to solve your own problems as long as they don't affect other departments (A)	Problems will be worked out in a policy committee so that no one person bears the brunt of the blame if things go wrong (S)

This company has never had a layoff (S)	This company has a fitness program you are encouraged to use, with excellent recreational facilities (L)
Your job seems to change every day. Often you have to become an instant expert to pull it off (M)	The work is good, but not very challenging. You can count on a stable future and some advancement (S)
A very old, reliable company offers you a good position (S)	A new company has a few rough spots, but the growth potential is outstanding (G)
$40,000 a year as an assistant, associate, gofer (P)	$35,000 a year with a direct hand in the policymaking process (C)
The best wage scale in the industry, a conservative company otherwise (P)	A decent wage and chance to try out many new ideas (M)
Final say on all financial operations in this company (A)	More money, but final say rests with the owner, who likes to pull rank occasionally (P)
This company has grown overnight and appears to be still zooming ahead; you'll go up fast (G)	A more sedate operation offers a considerably higher salary (P)
A merit pay raise and annual cost of living increase are guaranteed (S)	Raises based only on performance and about 40 percent of the employees do not receive a raise each year. You will directly control your division (C)
A job in the accounting department with three people working under you (C)	More money because you do all the accounting, but it is under someone else's management (P)
This company works only half a day on Fridays (L)	This company stands behind its salesmen and will uphold any commitments you make (C)

29

You will be in charge of your own projects from planning to finish (C)	This company does state-of-the-art projects years ahead of anyone else but is highly controlled (M)
You open a new office for a chain operation and hire all new personnel under your direction but follow company routines otherwise (C)	You will be part of a team heading a new division that seems likely to outsell the parent company in five years' time (G)
This company is working on a revolutionary new technique. You will have unlimited opportunity to try any processes and materials you want without cost controls if the project director sees merit in the idea (M)	This consulting company solves application problems for varied types of clients. Most of the problems are familiar to you and easy to solve. You do not have to report to anyone else what you intend to try; just file a completion report at the close (A)
You usually work on your own without clearing your decisions on routine matters with your supervisor (A)	Your company keeps meticulous records that require justifying everything you do in writing; the chances for advancement and training are outstanding (G)
Everyone who performs above average here is rewarded with a bonus, extra time off, a week's paid lunches in the nearby restaurant, or some other pleasant surprise (R)	The suggestion system at this company is really effective. You can make proposals for your own department, someone else's, or the whole company at any time. They are seriously reviewed and, if approved, you get to be in charge of carrying out the changes (M)
No two days are quite alike; you not only use all your training but have to be creative as well to stay on top (M)	A nice place to work; the pace is laid back and you never get stuck working late. You get to know what to expect from each customer pretty soon (L)
This job offers you several paths for advancement, depending upon what skills you develop (G)	This job offers you exceptional leave benefits—three weeks' vacation the first year, a month the second year, and bonus time off for many other reasons (L)

Adding It Up

Go down the margin by each pair of jobs and write the letter in parentheses for the job you chose. Count the number of times you chose each letter.

A =   L =   G =

C =   S =   X =

R =   M =   P =

Interpretation

It should be obvious that these selections compare the job features you ranked in Exercise 5. How do your scores compare?

Enter the number of:

A's by Autonomy _____
R's by Recognition _____
G's by Growth _____
C's by Authority _____
L's by Leisure _____
(There is no letter for clear guidance.)

S's by Security _____
P's by Pay _____
M's by Challenge _____
X's by Responsibility _____

Which feature got the highest score? Put a *1* in front of it on the following list. Put a *2* in front of your next-highest score and so on.

In the case of a tie, put all the ranks in front of each tying feature. For instance, if Pay and Leisure tied for first, either one could be in the first or second place so put a *1/2* in both spots. If you get to fifth place and three items tie put *5/6/7* in front of all three.

_____ Autonomy   _____ Security

_____ Pay   _____ Being recognized

_____ Challenging work   _____ Opportunity to grow

_____ Responsibility   _____ Leisure time—I work to live

_____ Clear guidance   _____ Power or authority

In a circle after each feature write the number of the rank you gave that feature in Exercise 5. Are you holding consistently in your job values?

Exercise 7
Your Special Characteristics

Pick five adjectives to describe your appearance (happy, pretty, sloppy, energetic, etc. . . .)

_____   _____
_____   _____
_____

Pick five adjectives to describe you as a worker (reliable, uncertain, meticulous, etc. . . .)

_____   _____
_____   _____
_____

Pick five adjectives to describe you as you deal with others (cooperative, bossy, etc. . . .)

_____   _____
_____   _____
_____

Pick five adjectives (or phases) to describe your performance to date (successful, disappointing, effective, etc. . . .)

_____   _____
_____   _____
_____

Pretend you are a friend writing a letter of recommendation for you to a prospective employer. Have the friend describe you to the employer, and work in all the points your adjectives suggest. Find a way to handle the negatives diplomatically.

Letter of Recommendation

Chapter 3

YOU'VE GOT WHAT IT TAKES

Before you get too far deciding what you want to do—what can you do now? Even if you want a job that will teach you many new skills, you'll have to come in the door knowing something. You may be looking for a job, but employers are looking for someone who can *do* the job.

Job applicants can err on both sides in assessing their skills. While a few brag too much, many don't give themselves enough credit. This chapter will help you hit the true middle ground.

Every skill has a range. The main reason people overlook or undervalue their skills is that they count only the peaks of expert performance. Look at it this way: if you went out in the backyard and practiced the broad jump, you would have an answer to the question "How far can you jump?" No matter what the world record is, no matter how often you fell on your behind, no matter that you never entered a real meet—you'd just answer 9 feet 6 inches (or whatever your best leap happened to be).

You should measure your job skills the same matter-of-fact way. Like the 9-foot 6-inch jump, if you ever did it once it's your skill level.

In this chapter, you'll construct a long resume consisting of a series of work sheets on which you will enter specific details about your qualifications as an employee. The work will make you more sure of what you can do. Preparing your real resume is going to be a lot easier after you have done this. You'll also find it easier to think on your feet during interviews after you spend this time thinking about your good qualities.

An Easy Start

The concrete is much easier to pin down. Start with tools, machines, and equipment. What do you know? The first example may seem a little silly. Bear with it. It isn't half as simple-minded as you might believe. You will be shown how to turn it to your advantage.

Consider the common electric typewriter. The range of possible skills related to it runs:

1. I recognize it when I see it.
2. I understand what it's used for.
3. I can hunt and peck rough drafts.
4. I can touch-type a little.
5. I can touch-type fast (a measurable skill).
6. I can touch-type fast and accurately.
7. I can touch-type fast, accurately, and create attractive and correctly formatted documents even if no one tells me exactly what to do.
8. All of these and I can repair it too.
9. All of these and I can manage a typing pool efficiently.
10. I have designed a revolutionary typewriter now in production.
11. Never use one anymore, I'm into word processors and . . .

Obviously, you don't need to go to this extreme. Just write down on the Skill Level work sheet the most advanced skill level you have ever reached on various pieces of equipment or with various tools. If you are uncertain what that is, use this checklist:

I recognize it.

Understand its use or theory.

Use it somewhat.

Use it well.

Use and repair, maintain, alter, reformat, etc.

Plan, design, or manage its use within the company structure.

Create or design the tool itself.

Use something more advanced.

Now, what do people in your field routinely handle or need to understand that you haven't listed? This is where the silliness of the typewriter exercise begins to pay off. People entering the field from formal training or from a less modernized company may not be handling the industry-standard tools. List everything you should know about if you were a state-of-the-art expert.

Skill Level—Tools and Equipment

You have some shortfalls, don't you? Well, start turning them into gold. When you are doing your job-hunting research and interviewing, find out everything you can about these tools. At least try to achieve the "I'd recognize one and understand what it is for" level.

Every time you learn something about the tools of the trade you will sound that much smarter to your next interviewer. Your willingness to learn will do more to overcome lack of experience than anything else short of actually using the tool.

> **Replace lack of experience with knowledge.**

A Word for Liberal Arts Types/Managers/ Professionals, etc.

Did you sneer a little at all this talk about equipment and tools?

Every discipline uses tools. Even if you don't plan to use the hard pieces of equipment yourself, ignoring the field standards equals ignorance. How well can you manage what you don't understand? How can you realistically plan projects when you don't know what your producers face?

Halfway Between the Concrete and the Abstract

So far we interpreted tools to mean hardware. But "tools of the trade" also means things you can't touch or see. All fields have standard approaches to problem solving. For this part of your long resume write down what you know about:

Processes
Procedures
Analytical approaches
Standard practices
Techniques
Planning and designing

Make note of your level of accomplishment. Do this in your own words for now.

People Skills

What relationship have you had to others in the workplace, in volunteer work, or in various organizations? How you handle people is an important part of every job. While some jobs don't seem to require much contact with others, they really do in some way. How can you let others know what you're up to? Do you tell your customers or boss? Do you write a report? Even getting supplies and information takes you outside the circle of just you and your work.

Skill Level—Procedures and Standard Practices

Those who do not expect to deal with outsiders very often should still analyze these skills. The very fellow who spends the early part of his career in the backwoods tagging and identifying fish may become a program manager. With this advance, he'll likely end up talking to citizen groups, other scientists, and so on.

Here's a checklist of people skills. It includes activities with and without others, responsibilities taken and given away.

Follow orders
Explain orders
Follow guidelines
Train others
Assign tasks
Set guidelines
Allow others to work without interference
Trust others to do important jobs
Meet strangers who know my field
Meet strangers who aren't familiar with what I do
Work out details, plans, and compromises with my peers
Act as a liaison or negotiator between groups
Address groups informally
Persuade others to think, do, buy, etc.
Speak before the public
Supervise others
Manage a team
Motivate others
Advise others
Enhance other people's careers

You can think of more skills that fit what you can do.

Management Skills

You have already itemized some skills that are usually considered part of management. Now focus on the broader picture. Not managing people directly, but managing the work, the program, the company, and so on. What can you offer an employer that will make his or her company a success?

I like designing a program, or managing it in action, or carrying it out myself.

I can study a problem and come up with a workable solution.

I enjoy noticing an opportunity and devising a way for the company to use it.

I find ways to cut costs.

I find ways to increase production or efficiency.

I can get realistic prices and costs to achieve a goal.

I can set realistic schedules.

I can set a budget that works.

I can create profit in a new program or enhance it in an existing one.

Skill Level—People

I can enhance the department's/company's reputation.

I can make the most of people and their talents for the company's benefit.

That's the general idea. Once again, add related talents in your own words.

Skill Level—Management

The Top Is in Sight—Making Policy

Unless you are coming into a company at a very high level with considerable background, policy setting is not usually a skill you'd consider. In a small company or within a department, however, you might influence the prevailing attitudes, assumptions, and underlying reasons.

Even if you have never done this, could you do it? Think of policy as everything that influences the company's basic view of the outside world and how it should approach that world. Also count the usual way the company handles its own employees and internal matters.

Did you ever do anything that changed an organization's policy? Take credit for it. The ability to shape the very personality of an organization is the most powerful of all. This is a good reason for entry-level people to include volunteer work on their resumes.

What can you count? Count the time you talked your previous employer into setting up a reimbursement-for-training program. Count the time you helped persuade the city to hold public hearings only in locations accessible to the handicapped.

Did you ever work as a clerk in the complaint department of a rather nasty store? Well, did you change the way that store started treating its customers and train others to do the same? That's policy. You may not have made any policy decisions so far, but if you ever have, in any sphere, put it down.

If you have the talent to positively affect the whole orientation of an organization, you have the potential to go very, very far.

Skill Level—Policy

Putting Your Skills Back Together Again

List the places where you have worked so far, in chronological order. For each employer or volunteer organization list the details of the job. Now match those duties with the skills you just put down for yourself.

Are you entering a new career field? You will find that this exercise helps you demonstrate what you can do when your experience is short.

Can you prove your claims? Okay, beef up this resume. If you noted that you could create a project and manage it, put down the exact project(s) that you did create, manage, or carry out. Did you claim that you could recognize opportunity or enhance profits? Once again, put down specifically what you did on your various jobs that gives supporting evidence. Use measurable terms whenever possible—something like "decreased inventory by 15 percent without any increase in the number of items that were out of stock."

Jobs	Duties	Skills

Transferring Skills

Even under the same job title the work at company A will differ from what is done at company B. Some jobs have no exact counterpart elsewhere. Or, you may be starting a new career direction.

At this point, you should do Exercise 8. Look at it now.

The skills you isolated can go many places. If you are beginning a new career, list or find out what skills you will need in your new job. Look at the skills you have already used. There should be some matches. You will build your resume around these matches along with any special training you have taken for the new job.

Skills needed for new job:	Skills already used:
_____	_____
_____	_____
_____	_____
_____	_____
_____	_____
_____	_____
_____	_____
_____	_____
_____	_____
_____	_____
_____	_____
_____	_____
_____	_____
_____	_____
_____	_____
_____	_____
_____	_____
_____	_____

While you have this long list in front of you, circle a few of the highlights. You might as well glow in your accomplishments! Also take a look at the whole thing quickly. You will probably find that although different jobs had different duties, you put down the same skill groups many times. Transferring skills is the key to changing careers and meeting new opportunities.

Exercise 8
Your Skills List

List every duty you have performed in volunteer jobs, work, or school activities.

Break each one down into data/tools/things skills:

Manual skills	Managing skills
Other body skills	Planning skills
Thinking skills	Analytical skills
Coordinating skills	Persuasive skills
Organizing skills	Creative skills

Now write a more specific phrase for each skill that each duty took.

Notice which skills appear again and again. Even though the jobs were different, many of the skills overlap. They are what you take with you when you job-hunt. Your successes and failures really indicate skill levels in various actions or choices. As you can see, each duty involves several skills. Wherever you did a job badly, try to evaluate which skill was the weak link. Where you succeeded, which skill helped most?

Your Skills List

Exercise 9
Your Skills Resume

Follow the skills assessment routine described earlier in this chapter. From your long resume build a one-page skills resume of your most notable job-related skills.

Skills Resume

Exercise 10
Your Personal Time

Having a wildly exciting job and getting home from the office by five o'clock may not be compatible goals. What you are free to do now can become impossible with your new work schedule. You should make a realistic survey of how much personal time you are using before you take a new job.

How many hours do you spend per week on:

_____ hobbies

_____ recreation

_____ cultural activities

_____ routine appointments (such as weekly allergy shots)

_____ maintenance (laundry, car repairs, shopping)

_____ getting dressed, bathing, etc.

_____ eating (including fixing meals, grocery shopping)

_____ transportation

_____ time with family, friends

_____ other activities (volunteer work, church, meetings, etc.)

_____ sleep

What is your weekly total? _____

A week has only 168 hours.

You need to decide how flexible you can be, how much of this personal time is absolutely necessary to you.

Write the balance between career and personal life that will satisfy you. Put this information on the Career Connector.

But What Should You Have on the List?

The only reason you went through all this was to help yourself get a job. Knowing your talents is all to the good. But you really need to know if you have what it takes to get the job you want. You should now profile your target job or jobs. Compare what you need to be able to do (job profile) to the skills you already have (long resume and Career Connector).

Job Profile

The following information should be included for each job you are considering:

- Main duties/tasks
- Education/experience required: kind of degree, curriculum requirements, prior work experience, skills required

- Salary range: starting salary, earning potential
- Occupational setting: hours, travel, relocation, fringe benefits, physical environment
- Opportunities: organizations hiring, areas of country with job openings, projected outlook for the field, opportunities for advancement

Now, work at closing the gap between what you have and what you need.

You can begin this right away. You should continue updating the job profile as you learn more about it during your job hunt. When you talk through your network or go to interviews, learn as much as you can about the ideal traits and skills of the potential employee.

No interview will be a total waste for you. Take heart even when you are turned down. You are that much more ready for the next opportunity. And you will end up with a job. Use your interviews to ask questions about the job, the duties, the skills needed, the standard practices, the equipment, the training required.

> **New entrants: Focus on your general skills.**

To start your job profile, you can begin at the library by looking up a description of the job in the *Dictionary of Occupational Titles* (U.S. Department of Labor, Manpower Administration).

Express the job requirements in the same terms you used to assess your skills. Check off the ones you already have. By those, jot down the specific examples of proof you can give. Unless you are unique, you will have quite a few holes. These are skills you don't have. Now what?

Look at those skills you seem to lack. Do you really lack them, or have you just forgotten to put them on your list? Think whether there is any way you might have used those skills somewhere. Still no? Then the easiest way to put that skill in your resume is by knowledge. Remember the typewriter we began with. Surely you can develop the "I recognize it and I understand what it's used for" level of expertise.

> **Old hands: Focus on the specifics.**

This gives you yet another excuse to wrangle an interview somewhere. The employer who might not want to talk to yet another job hunter will probably appreciate your startling honesty. Don't worry so much about your imperfections. Be bold enough to say, "I'm looking for a job as a _____. I have some background, but I need to learn a lot about _____. Can I arrange a tour of the facility with someone knowledgeable and possibly get some advice on training while I'm at it?" You can't show much more initiative than that. If you lack experience, then initiative and eagerness to learn will count heavily.

Every old pro sees many inexperienced people over the course of a career. Sometimes the pro gets stuck training these newcomers. You could be a day brightener by showing up with a positive attitude. Besides that, the nicest people to work for are those who enjoy others' successes. People of this kind get excited about finding someone receptive to their enthusiasm for the job. Mentors are people who groom another person for success in their footsteps. Having a good mentor can really speed up your career. This is a very good way to find one. He or she is looking for you, too.

Developing New Skills

Regroup. At this point, if you've faithfully worked through all the exercises, you know the following things:

1. What you want to do (career objective)
2. What you can do (current skills)
3. What you should be able to do (job requirements)
4. As much as possible about the things you can't do that are part of your intended job

Earlier in this book you were told to substitute *knowledge* for lack of experience. That advice still holds, but now there is more: Get *experience*.

Recent graduates, people reentering the career world, and career changers face a special problem. You could get the right experience if you could get the job you want, but you can't get the job without experience. There *is* a way to break this vicious circle. It's not law school—sometimes resorted to as an act of despair. It's the back door. And you won't have to pay for the opportunity.

Remember how much it costs to go to law school or get an M.B.A., because the back door does have drawbacks. Namely, little or no money for your efforts. But the advantages are much greater. You do get valuable work-related experience. You do develop your skills. You get to try out your intended field before you marry into it. You will meet people who can help you find a job later on. You may even be invited to come in the front door as a regular professional employee.

The principal back doors are internships, volunteer work, temporary placement, and similar options.

Internships

The whole idea behind an internship is to introduce you to a specific career field or type of work environment. These can range from informal arrangements to highly structured programs. There are numerous sources for them. Look for these sources at libraries and guidance offices:

- *Directory of Washington Internships*
- *Directory of Undergraduate Internships*
- *Guide to Mass Media Internships*
- Formalized internships with local companies
- Alumni-sponsored internships
- Linkages through informational interviews, family, friends, etc.
- Programs through government agencies
- Notices in professional publications

If these sources don't lead you to an appealing internship, develop your own. Write down your objectives and the kind of experience you want. Present this to companies that interest you, along with a summary of your training and skills to date. Many, many companies are open to the idea of using interns. For them it can be an inexpensive way to get extra help. For you, it's a chance to guide your own experience.

Send the organizations a letter with the following information:

- An outline of your background (skills, work experience, activities, etc.)
- Reasons you would like to be an intern

- What you hope to gain from the experience
- Duties that you are willing to perform

Follow the letter up with a phone call one week later. Keep in touch until you get a definite response. You should address your letter and any phone calls to the person you would be working for—whoever makes the hiring decisions in the department you would work in. If the personnel office must become involved, let that person run interference for you.

You will get out of an internship what you put into it.

1. Find out what your responsibilities are before you start.
2. Talk to the internship director and discuss what you want to achieve.
3. Use your initiative.
4. Find out what various departments do.
5. Get to know the top decision makers.
6. Ask coworkers about their jobs.
7. Participate in professional activities (trade shows, meetings, lunches) whenever possible.

Volunteer Work

You can volunteer for almost any type of work. More important, companies that would not hire you on a regular basis because of your lack of experience may take you as a volunteer. Needless to say, you will do your very, very best to make a good impression. Two things can happen: you learn a lot that you need to know, or you prove your worth and get hired eventually.

Temporary Agencies

Registering with a temporary agency can expose you to a variety of jobs and companies. In this case, you will be paid for the time you put in.

To register with an agency, simply look in the yellow pages. Sign up with several agencies to improve your chances of getting around. Temporary agencies do not charge fees, and these assignments can lead into the real thing.

Adult Education Programs

Many communities provide these programs through local colleges or community centers. Instructors are often moonlighters from local businesses. If so, they are a good source of information about the field as it is practiced and may be able to lead you to a job opening if you are an impressive student. These classes are very inexpensive. Much, much less than law school. Faster, too. Typical courses rarely last more than eight weeks.

Self-Education

Here's an old idea back again. One of the most important steps you can take in a smart career hunt is to upgrade your command of the field you want to enter. Know the jargon, the standard operating procedures, the trends, the legal issues, etc., etc. This is critical. Any ignorance you care to preserve is likely to be your downfall. Especially during interviews.

Your grammar may be perfect, but if you respond to a question about "bluelines" like a wide-eyed beagle when interviewing for an editorial position, the interviewer will know you've never been near a publishing company. If international trade sounds exciting, for goodness' sake understand the term "GATT."

Read professional journals. Check out anything you can find on the field from your public library. Scan the business pages. Talk to people who are doing the kind of work you want to do.

Identify the skills and knowledge that you need and then devise a strategy to obtain them. You could use the following form to help keep track of your progress.

Self-Education Strategies

What I need to develop or know	Strategy	Date
Improve my business writing skills.	• check out a book on business writing	3/16
	• enroll in the AE class	3/20

Chapter 4

YOU KNOW SOMEBODY WHO KNOWS SOMEBODY

It's bad enough to have to ask for a job; at least it should be easy to find one. Want ads make the search seem simple. You know there's a spot and where it is. But so does everyone else, and you usually get lost in the crowd. Even if you're perfect for the job.

Employment Agencies

Maybe an employment agency could help. You should know one very important thing before you put a foot through the door. Agencies sell people. The person who works on your case is paid on commission: he or she will move the hot goods first. The average agency is the least help to the people who need help the most. Don't even consider paying for the service. If you get an overwhelming urge to wander in, make it very clear that you will consider only fee-paid jobs.

You can get into real trouble at agencies if you're careless. They will ask where you have looked for a job and what progress you've made. Just for your record? No way. They will immediately send out anyone on their lists who could fill the jobs you tracked down. Agencies do tend to keep their own people from knocking each other out of the ring. But that doesn't include you yet. Agents don't collect on a job you find for yourself—they won't be happy if you get it and will try to fill it with a paying customer.

So keep your hot leads a secret? Another bad move. Once you're under contract, you can be charged for any information they give you. Even if you had heard about it already. Maybe you could win the fight in court, but it isn't worth the risk.

Your best bet is to steer clear of employment agencies.

It is true that some companies always call agencies to fill their jobs. They do it so someone else can sort out the masses. If you find out about a job on your own, the decision makers will still talk to you.

There are three big differences between you and most employment agents.

1. They have had lots of practice.

2. They are looking on behalf of someone else.

3. They don't care as much about your future as you do.

That's it. We're going to cover practice in the self-search section. In this chapter you will learn to do everything an employment agency will do for you, and more.

Resumes and Cover Letters

Some people print resumes by the hundred and blitz the town with them. You'll need a resume sooner or later, and the next chapter will help you with it. But an unrequested resume doesn't very often hit home. It's just another piece of paper with someone's history on it. At the very least, you should call the persons you intend to send a resume to and let them know it's on the way.

People hire people. Hold the resume until you've made human contact. The exceptions are placement services and want ads that request a resume only. But you already know your chances in the want ad racket are slim. Another use for a resume is leaving one with friends and others who know you are looking. Since your friends probably don't know enough about your job skills to help you much without a fact sheet, they'll be better prepared if they hear of an opening.

Placement Services

For a fee, this can be a good deal. You will have the best luck if you have readily identifiable job skills that are in some demand. The costs are modest since the services operate to benefit employer subscribers. An example is the Association of Association Executives. You give them a check and a resume; they pass your resume to employers with appropriate job openings. The employer gives you a call if interested. Because the service gives the employer only a few on-target resumes, your chances of being called are pretty decent. Similar services are available in many fields; track them down through professional and trade organizations.

Services like this operate in a very straightforward way. If you aren't sure what category of job you are looking for, don't have any pertinent experience, or are changing careers, don't expect much help. If you were fired or laid off, however, you would usually get a better chance here than at an employment agency.

Doing It Yourself

You know that perfect strangers won't of their own accord cross the street and whisper a tip about a hot job opening. What you may not know is that there *is* a way you can get good tips, even from a perfect stranger.

Don't count anyone out!

Don't look alone. Start with people you know: you probably know more people than you realize. Even a fairly shy person is on how-do-you-do terms with:

1. Parents
2. Brothers and sisters
3. Aunts, uncles, and cousins
4. Close friends
5. Acquaintances
6. Barbers, bartenders, salesclerks, and other service providers
7. Coworkers
8. People who contact your organization but don't work there
9. For students—other students, professors, teachers, and advisers
10. People with whom you have worked in community organizations or clubs

If you know two people in each of just nine of these categories, that's eighteen people who can think about finding a job for you.

But each of these people knows eighteen more. At least. And each of those knows another eighteen. By now, theoretically, you could have 5,832 people concerned with your job hunt. Who knows what they will hear?

To get help like that, though, you have to say, "I'm looking for a job," and say it loud and clear. Lots of people grumble about job hunting on bad days, and no one pays much attention. Be unmistakable and positive. Five thousand people won't run out and ask around—they'll just go on with their daily lives, but some of them will hear something and remember you.

Networking

The procedure just described was networking. Trendy term. Sounds very upscale. It isn't. It isn't even very sophisticated. But it does work. All you need to do is work it a little smarter.

The first rule has already been covered: be unmistakable. Your network won't net a job opening if people think you're just daydreaming.

The next rule is to get to more than those first eighteen people. Get used to telling people you're job hunting. Tell people at parties. Especially tell people who are working in places like the one you want to work for.

The next rule is to keep records. That's because you're going to start reaching people you don't know very well (and some you don't know at all). Start up a network filing system using index cards. On the top of the card write the contact's name, job title, address, and phone number. Whenever you contact this person, note on the card the date, the topic/nature of communication, and the outcome of the interaction.

If you harbor any trace of snobbishness, get rid of it. The janitor in your building may know more than you do about what is going on at a place you'd like to work.

Questions to Ask Your Network Contacts

- Do you think my resume is suitable for this type of position?
- Do you belong to a professional association? How can I get in touch with the local chapter?
- Can you suggest sources where I might obtain job listings or announcements for this type of work?
- What local firms are most likely to have these kinds of positions?
- Do you know of organizations that offer formal training for this kind of work?
- Can you suggest directories and other print resources about employers in this field?
- Can you refer me to others in the field who might be able to provide me with additional assistance?
- Is there any other advice or information that you would like to add?
- May I contact you again if other questions arise?

Expanding Your Network

In addition to your shotgun announcement, you want to uncover people who can really give you inside information. You want to talk to people who hire people like you and people who have jobs like the one you want.

One way to get to those people is by using the informational interview. This kind of pre-job-hunting interview allows you to learn more about specific companies, employees, and their environment in a low-pressure situation. Unlike in the real job interview, what you don't know won't count against you. The greatest advantage of the informational interview is that you lay important groundwork for your job campaign and meet people who will know how to help you later on.

The informational interview is not a scheme to get you in the door to talk to an employer about a job. Talking to people about the field you are interested in is different from job interviewing. It is less formal and more informative, since neither you nor the person you are talking with is evaluating the discussion for the purpose of making an employment decision. Instead, there is an even exchange of information that is open and candid.

Get those names you need (by referrals or from directories), call them, and make an appointment. Ask if you can talk to them for 15 to 25 minutes in person.

Remember, your purpose is to gather information... not to ask for a job. Be prepared—have your questions ready.

Especially remember that this is your goodwill tour of the job world. Don't cheat. Something is going to look fishy if the first thing you do when you come in the door is hand out your resume—you are supposed to be gathering information. And don't outlast your welcome.

Many fields are very close. You'll find that professionals in some organizations know their counterparts from coast to coast and talk to each other more frequently than you would imagine. Sly tactics now won't look good later when they compare notes.

The following questions are some of the things you might ask during an informational interview. Use a little sense. The crusty old fellow who prides himself on practical knowledge is apt to find "Trace your career path for me" rather ridiculous. If you want to know, ask him how he "got into this line of work."

Informational Interview Questions

Job Description

1. What is your job title?
2. What is a typical day on the job like for you?
3. What percent of your time do you spend each day in various activities of your work?
4. What is the title of the person that you report to?
5. How free are you to do your work as you want to?
6. Where are you located in a normal working day?
7. What types of problems are you likely to face in a day's time?
8. What are the most satisfying and the most frustrating parts of your work?
9. What salary can one in an entry-level position expect in this field?

Advancement

1. How did you get to your current position?
2. What kind of entry-level jobs do you think are good training grounds for a person entering this field now?
3. What are the trends and developments in the field that you see affecting the career of someone just entering the occupation?

Preparation

1. How did you prepare for this occupation? What do you recommend for a person entering this occupation now?
2. What education/degrees/training/licenses are required? If not required, which are recommended?

3. What courses do you suggest for an undergraduate as preparation?

4. What are the best places to go for education/training for a position like yours?

5. If you could start all over again in launching your career, what steps would you take?

Life-style

1. What hours do you normally work?

2. Is overtime common?

3. In what ways is travel a factor in this job?

4. What are the professional organizations in this field?

5. How do they serve members?

6. What are the pressures that you contend with?

7. How does this occupation affect your private life?

8. What other things are expected of you outside of working hours?

Follow-Through

The finishing cap to networking is in the follow-through. Always, always, drop a thank-you note to the person who took time out from work to talk to you. Even if he or she was a grouch the whole time! Even if the interview was dreadful! That could have been a bad day, or a test, or anything. Maybe the person is a genuine grouch—but don't overlook the fact that you were not applying to work for that person but only seeking information that might lead you to someone else you would enjoy working for.

Always keep good records, too. Some of the little things you find out can really help you later on. Finally, rework your list of contacts routinely. This will help build the kind of relationship that makes people remember you when something does come up. It also establishes that you are serious and thorough—good traits. Be consistent, however, not a pest.

Cold Calling

More investigation on your part can expand your network considerably. Most jobs still go to people who show up at a good time and ask for them. When you don't have any idea that a job is available or any kind of introduction to the organization, you need to make cold calls.

Maintain your sense of pride and integrity here. Just because you got the name from a phone book doesn't mean you should slink in shamefacedly.

Before beginning your search for companies retreat a minute. Go back to Exercise 9, the personal skill summary exercise you have already done. The more broadly used your skills, the more valuable this exercise can be to you. A specialist in public relations or auditing can work in thousands of places. Focus your search then.

You can track down company names from the following sources:

1. The yellow pages

2. The business news section of a newspaper

3. Trade and professional journals
4. Directories available in a public or college library—several are listed at the end of this chapter
5. Dun and Bradstreet listings if you have access to them or know someone who does
6. *Commerce Business Daily*—look in the awarded contracts section to see who is doing what for the government
7. The chamber of commerce
8. Suppliers (printers, for example, can tell you who might be looking for a new graphics designer)
9. Local news pages of a newspaper
10. Volunteer organizations and clubs related to your interests
11. Government agencies—a manager who hires services can tell you what companies are out there and maybe how reputable they are
12. Conventions and trade shows—even if you can't afford to register, the exhibit area is usually wide open
13. Professional organizations, associations, leagues, boards, etc.
14. College placement offices—if you don't live near your alma mater or don't have one, try the local community college
15. The state or city unemployment office—even the employed can browse through the job listings. Listings in Washington, D.C., include numerous openings for the computer field and researchers with postdoctoral training, for example.

Launching the Job Search

When you have conducted the informational interviews, you will be ready to start your job hunt in earnest. Call the people you interviewed then and let them know you are looking for real now; they may be able to give you specific job leads. Go talk to these people again. Your purpose has now changed. In your first discussion, you simply sought information to clarify career goals. You are now seeking advice on finding appropriate opportunities.

Don't be discouraged if the first several people tell you they can't help. The main thing is to keep talking to people. Sooner or later someone will lead you to the right door. Maybe even one of the people who didn't have much to offer the last time you spoke. You are going to be a professional in your chosen field someday soon—start acting like one now: keep in touch with the other pros.

Present yourself to these potential employers as you really are. Obviously you want to put your skills and abilities in the best terms, but admit to your need for help. Ask for advice whenever you meet someone who seems open, sincere, and interested. Those people you are admiring from afar for their esteemed positions are probably asking each other for advice behind closed doors, too. They will consider your questions a sign of good sense and well-placed humility.

Scheduling Interviews

As for scheduling an actual interview, arrange interviews with organizations that appeal to you, whether or not you know a vacancy exists. You can send the company a cover letter with your resume and follow this up with a phone call. The best approach, however, is to *start* with a phone call.

Talk with the person who has the power to hire you, not someone in the personnel department. Personnel staff do not create new openings but fill existing ones. They are often the last to know about *future* job openings.

Making cold calls to schedule interviews can be quite nerve-racking. However, the reason that it is so stressful for most people is that they imagine that they will be either accepted or rejected, yes or no, cut-and-dried.

You are going to take a different, more positive approach. When making your calls, you will have one of three objectives in mind:

1. To arrange an interview
2. To schedule a time to talk with the employer further on the phone
3. To get a referral

By using the following script or a variation of its format, you will accomplish one of these three objectives 90 percent of the time.

Begin your call with a brief introduction:

> *Good morning [employer's name]. My name is _____ . I have considerable [occupational field] background/experience. Have I caught you at a good time?*

You don't want to ask if you're catching someone at a bad time. When you do this, you're offering the employer an excuse to say yes.

Your next step is to spark the employer's interest. Select a work-related skill or ability that you are especially proud of. Your voice will reflect your enthusiasm.

> *As the fund-raising chairman of XYZ committee, I supervised a team of forty and raised over $10,000 for ABC cause.*

Then go on to say:

> *The reason I am calling, [employer's name], is that I am looking for a new challenge and opportunity. Having researched your company, I would like to meet with you. I will be in your area this Thursday and Friday. Which day would be better for you?*

By ending your statement in this way, you are not giving the employer the opportunity to turn you down with a yes or no answer. You are simply offering a couple of alternatives for the employer to choose from.

You are likely to get one of three responses from the employer:

1. The employer will agree to meet with you.
2. The employer will display interest by asking you questions.
3. The employer will be unreceptive (and say the company is not hiring, send me your resume, etc.).

If you get the third response, you'll be ready to handle these roadblocks and still achieve one of your objectives!

If the employer asks you to send your resume:

> *I would be happy to, [employer's name]. So that I can be sure that my qualifications fulfill your needs, what skills are you looking for in this position?*

Now when you do send your cover letter and resume, you can draw attention to the specific skills *the employer* considers to be important.

If the employer doesn't have time to talk with you on the phone or to see you in person:

I understand that you are very busy. Perhaps I could call back at a better time. Are mornings or afternoons better for you?

Once again, you end your statement with an either/or question with the purpose of eliciting a positive response from the employer.

If the employer tells you that he or she is not interested or that the company does not have any openings:

I am really interested in your company. Are you planning any expansion in the near future that would create an opening?

If the employer still raises objections, you can still ask for a referral.

Do you know anyone in the field who might need someone with my skills and experience?

Why Some People Get Jobs

Even though you have good qualifications and a superior interviewing style, you won't get a job unless:

1. You are looking.
2. You are looking at the right time.
3. You seem interesting.

Timing is very important, but you won't know when to strike except by looking. Just live with the fact that the more actively you search and the more thoroughly you follow up and follow through, the better your chances. As for being interesting, that is a matter of letting other people know you are a serious can-do person. Work to create that impression from the moment you call. If you have no real work experience in the field but just finished training, identify yourself as a doctor, lawyer, Indian chief, or whatever, just as though you had done it for years. If you just got fired from a job as a systems analyst you are still a systems analyst—say so.

The topic isn't quite closed. You will need to keep practicing your search skills throughout your job-hunting days. You will find more help in looking interesting in person in the chapter on interviews. Chapter 5, on resumes, will help you look more interesting on paper.

Directories and Reference Sources You Should Know

General

Who's Who in America—many variations on this theme; you may be able to find the person you have an interview with listed somewhere

Dun and Bradstreet Reference Book of Corporate Management

The Social Service Organization and Agency Directory—includes state, federal, professional, and nonprofit organizations

National Trade and Professional Associations of the U.S.

Encyclopedia of Associations of the U.S. and Canada—gives names of executive officers

Consultant's News and *Management Consultant Guide*—both from Harvard Business School

Consultant's and Consulting Organization Directory

Job Bank

Value Line Investment Survey—appraises trends and forecasts growth in various industries

Directories in Print—help finding more help

Dun and Bradstreet Business Information Reports—not available through libraries—you must know someone with a subscription

Moody's Manuals—seven manuals by business type, including history, operations, products, officers, and financial reports

Standard & Poor's Corporation Records—like *Moody's* with daily supplements

Directory of Corporate Affiliations—lists affiliates and subsidiaries of 40,000 companies; can help you find a back door

F&S Index United States—cumulative and weekly summary of news articles from nearly 800 business publications

Business Periodicals Index

Business Index

100 Best Companies to Work for in America

By Interest Area

The following reference section provides lists of resources categorized by interest area.

ANTHROPOLOGY

American Anthropological Association
1703 New Hampshire Avenue, NW
Washington, DC 20009
202-232-8800

ART

Art Yellow Pages

Careers in the Arts: A Resource Guide

American Council for the Arts
570 Seventh Avenue
New York, NY 10018
212-354-6655

National Association of Artists' Organizations
1007 D Street, NW
Washington, DC 20002
202-544-0660

COMMUNICATIONS

The Standards Directory of Advertising Agencies: The Agency Redbook

American Marketing Association
250 S. Wacker Drive, Suite 200
Chicago, IL 60606
312-648-0536

Public Relations News
127 East 80th Street
New York, NY 10021
212-879-7090

American Advertising Federation
1400 K Street, Suite 1000
Washington, DC 20005
202-898-0089

American Association of Advertising Agencies
666 Third Avenue
New York, NY 10017
212-682-2500

Public Relations Society of America, Inc.
Career Information
845 Third Avenue
New York, NY 10022
212-826-1750

National Cable Television Association
1724 Massachusetts Avenue, NW
Washington, DC 20036
202-775-3550

CONSULTING/STARTING YOUR OWN BUSINESS

How to Run a Small Business

Jobs: How People Create Their Own

Association of Managing Consultants
500 N. Michigan Avenue, Suite 1400
Chicago, IL 60611
312-266-1261

American Association of Political Consultants
c/o Currell Associates, Inc.
320 N. Larchmont Boulevard
Los Angeles, CA 90004
213-466-3445

Small Business Administration
800-433-7212 (for information on its more than 300 publications)

DESIGN

American Art Directory

ECONOMICS

American Economic Association
1313 21st Avenue South, Suite 809
Nashville, TN 37212
615-322-2595

EDUCATION

Education Directory: Public School Systems in the United States

The Handbook of Private Schools

Teaching Abroad

American Federation of Teachers
555 New Jersey Avenue, NW
Washington, DC 20005
202-879-4400

National Education Association
1201 16th Street, NW
Washington, DC 20036
202-879-4400

ENVIRONMENTAL/LIFE SCIENCES

Conservation Directory (National Wildlife Federation)

Opportunities in Environmental Careers

Life Sciences Jobs Handbook

Ecology and Your Career

Department of Labor, Bureau of Labor Statistics
Washington, DC 20212

GEOLOGY

American Institute of Professional Geologists
17828 Vance Drive, Suite 103
Arvada, CO 80003
303-431-0831

GOVERNMENT

Federal, State, Local Government Directory

Washington Information Directory

United States Government Manual

Federal Job Information Office
800-555-1212

Department of State
Equal Employment Opportunity Office
Room 4421
Washington, DC 20520

American Planning Association
1776 Massachusetts Avenue, NW
Washington, DC 20036
202-872-0611

International City Management
 Association
1120 G Street, NW
Washington, DC 20005
202-626-4600

HEALTH

National Health Directory

American Health Planning
 Administration
1110 Vermont Avenue, NW, Suite 950
Washington, DC 20005
202-861-1200

American Physical Therapy Association
111 N. Fairfax Street
Alexandria, VA 22314
703-684-2782

American Occupational Therapy
 Association
1383 Piccard Drive, Suite 301
Rockville, MD 20850
301-948-9626

Health Science Communication
 Association
6105 Lindell Boulevard
St. Louis, MO 63112
314-725-4722

National Health Council
622 Third Avenue, 34th Floor
New York, NY 10017
212-972-2700

HISTORY

Organization of American Historians
112 N. Bryan Street
Bloomington, IN 47408
812-855-7311

HOTELS

American Hotel and Motel Association
888 Seventh Avenue
New York, NY 10019
212-265-4506

HUMAN RESOURCES

Training and Development Journal,
 published by the American Society for
 Training and Development

Training Magazine
612-333-0471

Personnel Administrator
216-826-4790

American Society of Personnel
 Administration
606 N. Washington Street
Alexandria, VA 22314
703-548-3440

National Labor Relations Board of
 Professionals Association
1717 Pennsylvania Avenue, NW
Washington, DC 20570
202-254-9192

American Association for Counseling and
 Development
5999 Stevenson Avenue
Alexandria, VA 22304
703-823-9800

American Society for Training and
 Development
P.O. Box 1443
1630 Duke Street
Alexandria, VA 22313
703-683-8100

JOURNALISM

Columbia Journalism Review

Washington Journalism Review

American Society of Journalists and
 Authors
1501 Broadway, Suite 1907
New York, NY 10036
212-997-0947

LANGUAGE

American Association of Language
 Specialists
1000 Connecticut Avenue, NW, Suite 9
Washington, DC 20036
301-762-6174

LAW

American Bar Association
750 N. Lake Shore Drive
Chicago, IL 60611
312-988-5000

Law and Society Association
University of Denver
1900 Oliver Street
Denver, CO 80220
303-871-6306

MANAGEMENT

American Management Association
American Management Association Building
135 West 50th Street
New York, NY 10020
212-586-8100

MUSEUMS

The Official Museum Directory

Directory of Private, Nonprofit Preservation Organizations

American Association of Museums
1225 I Street, NW, Suite 200
Washington, DC 20005
202-289-1818

PERFORMING ARTS

Musical America International Directory of the Performing Arts

Theater Directory

Opportunities in Acting

PHILOSOPHY

American Philosophical Society
104 South Fifth Street
Philadelphia, PA 19106
215-627-0706

PHOTOGRAPHY, FILM, AND BROADCAST MEDIA

Audio Visual Market Place: A Multimedia Guide

International Motion Picture Almanac

International Television and Video Almanac

Photographers Market

Production Company

The Student Guide to Mass Media Internships

PSYCHOLOGY

American Psychiatric Association
1400 K Street, NW
Washington, DC 20005
202-682-6262

American Psychological Association
1200 17th Street, NW
Washington, DC 20036
202-955-7600

National Association for Mental Health
1221 22nd Street, NW
Washington, DC
202-296-2149

PUBLISHING

American Book Trade Directory

Cabell's Directory of Publishing Opportunities

Journalism Career and Scholarship Guide

Literary Market Place

Magazine Industry Market Place

Editors and Publishers Weekly

SALES

National Retail Merchants Association
100 West 31st Street
New York, NY 10001
212-244-8780

Sales and Marketing Executives International
6151 Wilson Mills Road, Suite 200
Cleveland, OH 44143
216-473-2100

SOCIOLOGY/SOCIAL WORK

Social and Behavioral Sciences Job Handbook: The Insider's Guide for Specialists in Society and Human Behavior

Social Service Organizations and Agencies Directory

Public Welfare Directory

National Association of Social Workers
7981 Eastern Avenue
Silver Spring, MD 20910
301-565-0333

TRAVEL

Travel Industry Monthly

ASTA Travel News
212-826-9464

Travel Industry Personnel Directory

Travel Industry Association of America
1123 21st Street, NW
Washington, DC 20036
202-293-1433

Major Periodicals Listing Job Openings

Advertising Age

Agricultural Record

American Bar Foundation Research Journal

American Economic Review

American School and University

American School Board Journal

Architectural Record

Audio-Visual Instruction

Aviation Week and Space Technology

Barron's

BioScience

Black Scholar

Broadcasting

Business Week

Chemical Engineering

Chronicle of Higher Education

College Placement Annual

Computing

Editor and Publisher

Educational Researcher

Electronic News

Engineering News-Record

Environmental Science and Technology

Fortune

Journal of Accountancy

Journal of Housing

Mechanical Engineering

Modern Plastics

Nation

Nation's Health

Nature

New Scientist

New York Times

Oil and Gas Journal

Personnel Journal

Product Marketing

Public Management

Science

Textile World

Wall Street Journal

Washington Post

Writer's Digest

Chapter 5

WOULD YOUR OWN MOTHER RECOGNIZE YOU?

If your own mother looks at your resume and asks, "Who's this?" you could be defeating your purpose. Put simply, on paper, most people sound too much alike.

You wouldn't believe how many people resort to paying a fortune for cookie cutter resumes. Buy a nice dinner for two and do your own resume. You're the only one that's you, anyway, and the object should be to stand out from the crowd, not to join a mob. We'll give you some tips on format, types, and wording to keep you within bounds. You provide the background and personality.

What's So Hard About Resumes?

What you must realize is that a resume is a written inventory that concisely, but forcefully, describes your qualifications for a position. The purpose of your resume is to spark the potential employer's interest enough to learn more about you in person—to secure an interview.

You have done several exercises that helped you build an accurate assessment of your strengths and weaknesses. Leave out the weaknesses. Then decide what to put in.

It is very difficult to summarize your life experience on a piece of paper. You can go about this task in several ways.

1. Write down everything about your previous experience.
2. Discuss your past with a counselor or friend, put the material together, and draft a resume.
3. Begin with the type of job you are seeking.

The third option is the most effective and practical way to focus your resume on what's really important.

- Write out your job objective (field of interest, company type, skills you want to use, etc.).

Job Objective

- Imagine yourself in the role of an employer hiring for the position described in your objective.
- Brainstorm the qualifications (skills, abilities) that as an employer you would be looking for in an employee.

Qualifications

- Select one of those qualifications and quickly scan your past life, work, and education for experiences where you developed or demonstrated those skills.
- Select one of those experiences and describe it in detail, answering the following questions:

> What did you do?
> How did you do it?
> What was the result?

Experience That Built Qualifications

Your resume will now match the job you are going after. If you are interested in two diverse fields, you should develop a resume targeting each. You needn't develop a different resume for each interview—it is too time-consuming and expensive. Once you have drafted your resume, ask someone in that field to critique it.

Presentation

Before you agonize over colored paper, fancy texture, and typesetting versus printing, consider this: the most important thing about a resume is to make it neat and make it businesslike. If you want colored paper, okay. Just be sure it's a very pale color, and a neutral—cream, gray, beige, off-white—not green, pink, or lavender. Possibly you can use a blue, a very pale blue.

> **Buy a nice dinner, and do your own resume.**

Paper comes in several weights and textures. You want 20-pound bond if you can find it. If not, use 15-pound. Just be sure it feels substantial; some rag content will help. You will probably have to get your paper at an office supply store; drugstores don't usually carry paper of this quality.

Typed or printed? The question isn't worth much fuss. What you put on your resume matters much more. For some jobs, such as graphics design, the ability to choose and use typefaces well is one of the skills you should be able to demonstrate. So typeset and print if you want. Usually, a typewritten resume is perfectly fine, as long as it is clean and error-free and the typewriter was good. Having your resume on a word processor is a real luxury. You can easily reword a passage here and there to fit different jobs.

Resume Types

The types are boundless, but three basic formats are normal: chronological, functional, and combination. They will cover everything you need to know.

The *chronological resume* lists your jobs in order, with the current or most recent one at the top, working down to the most remote.

The *functional resume* categorizes skills you believe to be the most important in the job that you are seeking.

The *combination resume* combines the chronological and functional resumes. It is a summary of your skills followed by a description of one or two relevant job experiences.

Basic Parts of the Resume

Personal Information

Include your full name, followed by your address and phone number. It is *not* necessary to include your age, marital status, height, weight, health status, or photo.

Objective

Usually it is pretty worthless—everyone knows you are looking for a job. A challenging position with room to grow? Well, who doesn't want that? It's so pat that it's meaningless. If you don't have anything more specific to say, omit this element from your resume. If you plan to send your resume to large companies or have strong feelings about features you are looking for, then do put your objective in.

Your Work History

Functional resumes sometimes omit this. If you do a functional resume, at least put down the names of the companies you worked for and the dates so that the employer can tell whether you started yesterday or have solid experience. Include the name of the company, location, dates employed, and job title. Offer a brief description of duties and responsibilities. Quantify these whenever you can (dollar amount of merchandise you sold, number of people you supervised, percentage of increased production, etc.).

Education

Include name of school, degrees and dates received, or dates of attendance. (Optional: academic honors, relevant activities.)

References

Every office drawer has a file full of resumes that say, "References available on request." Yes, it is the standard format. But it isn't particularly smart. Companies vary. Some will need to fill a position in a crunch—consulting firms, for example. Employers under pressure automatically go toward the people who make life simplest and give their references up front. Other employers favor the personal interview and won't care about your references at all.

Remember this. The personnel officer and the decision maker live in two different worlds. Personnel offices are administrative bailiwicks. The typical work load consists of record keeping above all else. Here lie the company's retirement plans, lists of anniversary dates, insurance forms, licenses, etc. Sending forms and waiting for others to send forms are part of the personnel officer's normal working day. In this world, "References available on request" fits right in.

Elsewhere, things may be quite different. The small agency that suddenly gets a big contract, the editorial consulting firm, the software design group, and the marketing department work under pressure and on deadline. In your job hunt, you should reach the working decision maker whenever possible—not the personnel office.

What "everybody" does is not the key. What the decision maker needs is the critical point.

We suggest a bold move. Give your references. Right away. Here are the advantages:

1. You don't create problems for the employer who's in a hurry.

2. You demonstrate that someone is willing to vouch for you.

3. You may push the right button.

The employer who looks at your references may see a name he or she recognizes. That may create a favorable impression, a familiarity that separates you from the pack. Professionals do tend to stick together. Don't be surprised if the bigwig in Minneapolis used to work with the Joe Smith you know in Mobile, Alabama.

Simply put your references on a separate sheet. You don't need to explain them at all on the resume itself. If you wish to do that, you may say, "References attached."

Focus only on relevant information that supports your career objective and PROOFREAD your resume!

The Words You Use

You have to make a choice; business gets carried away with certain words like "prioritize," "implement," "output," etc. Real English is much more lively. But for every employer who'll appreciate the straightforward language, you'll find a stick-in-the-mud who feels more secure with big words. Our recommendation is to use mostly regular English and throw in a piece of jargon or two just to show that you have done your research and know about the field.

Whatever words you pick, make them really work for you.

Paint clear pictures:

> Don't say, "Was given responsibility for. . . ."
>
> Say, "Took responsibility for. . . ."
>
> Better yet, "Controlled. . . ."

Sound like you are in charge of your career, not a puppet.

For additional help, consult the Action Word List that follows later in this chapter.

Cover Letters

Many recommend that you tailor your resume for each position that you seek. To avoid this, make good use of the cover letter. There you can focus on why you are the best person for a *specific* opening. The cover letter should be concise and tailored for an individual employer.

A cover letter should be no longer than three paragraphs.

Introduce yourself in the first paragraph. Mention the position you are seeking, how you heard about it, and why the particular organization appeals to you.

In the second paragraph, explain why you are interested in the company and why you are qualified for the position. Do not quote from your resume. Instead, provide further details that will impress the employer.

In the final paragraph, you should request an interview. The fastest way to get a response is to state that you will call within the next week.

Always type—or word process—the letter.

Examples of cover letters are shown at the end of this chapter.

Which Type Will Work for You?

There is no single, best format. However, certain formats are better than others, depending on your background and experience.

- **Chronological**

  + If you have made successful moves, worked for well-known or prestigious companies, and increased your responsibilities, use the chronological approach.

  – Chronological resumes can be dull, and they show employment gaps easily. This resume can make a lack of success rather obvious and may not provide enough evidence of skills.

- **Functional**

  + If you have little or no direct experience in the field, need to show what you can do, are trying to change career direction, lack a history of promotions, or have gaps in employment, the functional approach is your best bet.

  – Functional resumes are difficult for employers to interpret: it is not always clear at what level the person carried out the listed skills, or for how long, or whether the person succeeded. Also, some employers just do not like them.

- **Combination**

  + This resume may be the best solution. It highlights your abilities for the position you are seeking and also presents positions you have held where you've demonstrated these skills.

  Examples of the various types of resumes follow.

Chronological Resume

Mary Johnston
1350 James Avenue
Oakland, CA 94720
(415) 555-2323

EXPERIENCE:

<u>Program Director</u>, American College, Berkeley, California. Administer innovative experimental learning programs. Coordinate seminars and field placements for 300 graduates. Established and maintain faculty advisory board. (September 1986 to present)

<u>Coordinator</u>, Bank of Oakland, California. Coordinated, trained, and evaluated summer personnel in banking operations. Created and implemented cross-training program for summer staff.
(June 1984 to July 1986)

<u>Management Assistant</u>, Doff Corporation, Oakland, California. Reviewed employment applications. Devised and maintained informational record systems. Facilitated communications with staff, clients, and subcontractors. (January 1982 to September 1983)

EDUCATION:

University of California, Berkeley
M.A. English, June 1984
B.A. Psychology, June 1982

SPECIAL SKILLS:

Communication, organization, training, supervision, evaluation

REFERENCES

Chronological Resume for a Recent Graduate

Grace Smith
132 Rolling Lane
McLean, VA 22102
(703) 555-1058

EXPERIENCE:

Robinson's Clothing Store, Chapel Hill, North Carolina, September 1988 to May 1989. <u>Evening Manager</u>: recorded sales, assisted customers, responsible for inventory control, supervised two salesclerks.

Senator Jack Hughes, Washington, D.C., Summer 1984. <u>Program Assistant</u>: Performed a variety of duties relating to civil rights legislation. Coordinated constituent requests. Prepared media releases.

Abrec Company, Greensboro, North Carolina, Summers 1982-83. <u>Office Assistant</u>: Devised new filing system. Prepared annual reports. Facilitated communication between management and clients.

Personal Strengths: Problem solver, energetic, responsible.

EDUCATION:

B.A., May 1988, University of North Carolina at Chapel Hill
Major: Sociology

College Activities: Public Relations Club, Chairperson
                     Student Government Association,
                        Representative
                     Kappa Kappa sorority
                     Intramural athletics

REFERENCES

Functional Resume

ROBERTA BACARAC
115 Lincoln Street
Seattle, Washington 98105
Home: (206) 292-1567
Work: (206) 725-1932

EXPERIENCE

<u>Supervision of Children</u>: Playground Director responsible for care of 50 children. Supervised five playground aides. YMCA Swimming Instructor. Organized and taught three 10-week classes. Participated in Child Development Practicum. Observed and eventually aided teachers at a day-care facility for four hours per week. Part-time baby-sitter since high school.

<u>Program Planning</u>: Planned and coordinated an activities schedule as Playground Director, Created detailed lesson plans for swimming classes. Attended weekly planning sessions at day-care center during practicum and eventually was responsible for planning a total week activity schedule.

<u>Parent Relations</u>: Met with parents as a representative of the playground and swimming programs. Received comments and mediated any conflicts that occurred. As a College Orientation Leader, gained experience answering questions of concerned parents.

<u>Management/Supervision</u>: Managed a concession stand at an amusement park. Kept records, opened facility, and supervised other employees. As a hostess at a restaurant, coordinated employees, controlled reservations, and monitored flow of work. Observed duties and responsibilities of day-care operator during practicum.

EDUCATION

University of Washington, Seattle, Washington
B.A. in Home Economics, May 1986
Concentration: Human Development

<u>Related Courses</u>:
- Child Development
- Family Studies
- Family Sociology
- Parent-Child Interaction
- Marriage and Family Interaction
- Adolescent Behavior Seminar

<u>College Activities</u>:
- Orientation Assistant
- Intramural Sports
- American Home Economics Association
- Vice Governor of Residence Hall Floor

REFERENCES

Functional Resume for a Recent Graduate

Jeff Knight
1375 Lanover Street
Townsen, Maryland 21204
(301) 555-7999

SKILLS

Data Management	Executed data management and interactive programs to create large computer files in preparation for computer simulations.
Research	Consulted with investigators on specific research topics. Wrote periodic reports to summarize projects.
Laboratory	Performed analytical determinations of chemicals by chromatography. Synthesized organic compounds using fractionation and distillation techniques.

EDUCATION

University of Maryland College Park
BA, Biology, June 1989—Concentration: Cellular biology

SPECIAL PROJECTS

Volunteer instructor for independent biology class
Coordinated five-day seminar for freshman biology majors

EXPERIENCE

Lab Assistant, General Research, Biology Division, Fairfax, VA, Spring 1983

Waiter, Leon's Cafe, Baltimore, MD, Summers 1981, 1982, 1983

Combination Resume

JAMES COBAN
2399 South Road
Portland, Oregon 97208
503-555-5678

RESEARCH — Developed university and government surveys for sociology department of major university. Researched background material for articles appearing in major national mathematics journal.

EDITING — Directed day-to-day operations for the <u>Journal of Applied Math</u>. Handled all general queries with authors and served as liaison between authors and publishers.

FINANCIAL ANALYSIS — Analyzed quantity audits, projections, and financial statements of university department. Authorized expenditures of $175,000 budget.

MANAGEMENT — Responsible for smooth running of 15-person department. Prepared minutes and agenda for faculty and editorial meetings. Carried out administrative policies of section: processed payroll, coordinated work schedules and equipment. Interpreted and applied university and government policy.

Staff assistant to chairman, Department of Sociology, University of Oregon, 1974 to present.

Assistant to chairman of Mathematics Department. Portland State University, 1972-74.

Secretary/editor, <u>Journal of Applied Math</u>, 1970-71.

EDUCATION — B.A., Portland State University, 1971. Humanities major. Honor student.

REFERENCES

Combination Resume

Jane Tishner
231 Maple Street
Bloomington, Indiana 47401
812-555-5555 (home)
812-555-4545 (work)

GRAPHICS EXPERIENCE:	DESIGN. Designed logos and patches for athletic teams. Created advertising brochures and logo for food company. Designed all visual materials used by sorority for various events.

LAYOUT. Performed layout work for advertisements for food company. Coordinated layout of promotional posters for various student groups.

PROGRAM DEVELOPMENT. Planned publications and graphic division for steering committee of Indiana University Student Foundation.

WORK HISTORY:	Sales Clerk, Al's Art Studio, Cincinnati, Ohio, 1980-86.

Graphic Designer, Tower's Sporting Goods, Cincinnati, Ohio, Summer 1984.

Art Director, _Panache_, Elkhart, Wisconsin, Summer 1983.

EDUCATION:	B.A., Fine Arts/Graphic Arts
May 1986, Indiana University, Bloomington, Indiana

COLLEGE ACTIVITIES:	Indiana University Student Foundation
    Publications Coordinator, 1985-86
Alpha Alpha Sorority
    Art Director, 1983-86
Student Government
    Graphics Chairperson, 1984-86

REFERENCES

Reentry Resume

Karen Mathews
690 Meadow Lane
Cincinnati, Ohio 45220
513-555-4555

SKILLS

Word Processing: Wang OIS-140 system
Knowledge of mail merge, glossary, and text editing

Typing: 65 wpm

Shorthand: Gregg, 110 wpm

EDUCATION

James Secretarial Academy, 1960
Cincinnati, Ohio

Grant University, 1988
Cincinnati, Ohio
Continuing Education Courses
"Secretarial Sciences"
"Automated Office" (70 hours of Wang training)

WORK HISTORY

1984–1987	Free-lance typing: theses, legal documents
1960–1965	Dupont Systems, Cincinnati, Ohio

COMMUNITY ACTIVITIES

1970 to present: St. Paul's Women's Network

- Coordinate monthly newsletter
- Prepare all copy and layout
- Organize mailing and distribution
- Coordinate programs

REFERENCES

Reentry Resume

Janet Woods
201 South Cary Avenue
McLean, Virginia 22103
703-555-1098

SKILLS

- Interior Design:

  Ability to determine appropriate decorating designs for homes, apartments, and stores. Excellent color coordination; extensive knowledge of furniture styles. Sketches available.

- Building Renovation:

  Ability to secure, negotiate, and skillfully supervise the work of plumbers, painters, carpenters, and landscapers.

- Home Decorating:

  Full sewing capabilities. Design own patterns. Reupholster sofas and armchairs.

EDUCATION

Bradley University
B.A., Studio Art/Design, 1953
Graduated Cum Laude

RELEVANT SKILLS:

Photography, Painting, Applique

REFERENCES AND PORTFOLIO PROVIDED

Reentry Resume

Nora Lamee
145 Isenburle Drive
Santa Barbara, California 93105
805-555-5698

EDUCATION

M.A., Adult Education, George Washington University, 1988

B.S., Elementary Education, Brent College, 1964

EXPERIENCE

<u>English Tutor</u>: Provided individualized instruction to children in grades 2-7 (1977-1982)

<u>Elementary Teacher</u>: Developed curriculum for accelerated English program. Voted "Teacher of the Year" by New England Teachers Association. Green Briar Elementary School, Amherst, Massachusetts (1965-1967)

CERTIFICATION

Elementary Education, grades K-8. Massachusetts License.

Elementary Education, grades K-6. Virginia License.

REFERENCES

Action Word List

accomplish	decide	identify	participate	schedule
achieve	delegate	induce	perform	secure
add	demonstrate	influence	persuade	select
adjust	describe	inform	plan	sell
administer	design	initiate	predict	simplify
adopt	determine	illustrate	prepare	sketch
advise	develop	imagine	present	solve
advocate	diagnose	inspect	print	speak
allocate	differentiate	inspire	process	streamline
analyze	dispatch	install	produce	strengthen
appraise	dispense	instruct	program	succeed
approve	display	integrate	project	summarize
arbitrate	dissect	interpret	promote	supervise
arrange	distribute	interview	proofread	synthesize
assemble	document	invent	propose	systematize
assess	draft	investigate	publish	
assist	draw	involve		teach
attain			question	theorize
audit	earn	launch		train
	edit	lead	raise	transfer
budget	educate	lecture	recommend	translate
	effect	lobby	reconcile	treat
calibrate	encourage	locate	record	troubleshoot
care	enlist		recruit	
change	establish	maintain	reduce	update
check	estimate	manage	refer	upgrade
clarify	evaluate	map	regulate	
classify	examine	measure	rehabilitate	verify
coach	exhibit	mediate	reorganize	
code	explain	model	repair	write
collate	express	monitor	replace	
communicate		motivate	replenish	
compete	forecast		report	
compile	fulfill	navigate	represent	
complete		negotiate	research	
compose	generate		resolve	
compute	guide	observe	respond	
conduct		organize	revamp	
consolidate	hire	originate	review	
control			revise	
coordinate			rewrite	
counsel				
create				
critique				

Cover Letter

Jane Radkin
370 Ranch Drive
Denver, CO 80205

March 15, 1989

Mrs. Carol Jackson
Mott Enterprises
8330 Tenely Circle
Denver, CO 80214

Dear Mrs. Jackson:

Mr. Stan Naple, director of Naple Marketing International, suggested I write to you and apply for the position of research analyst. Please consider the enclosed resume as an application for this position.

My educational background in marketing and computer science, along with my quantitative skills, makes me especially qualified for the position. I work well independently and communicate easily with all types of people. My analytical skills have been demonstrated through experience in coding information for computer input and checking output for accuracy.

At your earliest convenience, I would appreciate discussing my qualifications with you. I will call you within the week to schedule an interview.

Sincerely,

Jane Radkin

Enclosure

Cover Letter

Sheila Farns
65 Florence Street
Coronado, CA 93466

April 25, 1989

Ms. Martha Main
Senior Employment Representative
General Systems, Inc.
19 Highland Avenue
San Francisco, CA 94660

Dear Ms. Main:

Dr. Fusilow, in the U.C. Santa Barbara Communications Department, has informed me of your company's expansion plans. Since you are extensively involved in dyadic communication research, I am very interested in an entry-level research position with your organization. I will receive my bachelor's degree in Communications from U.C. Santa Barbara in June, 1989.

I have performed three independent research studies at the Hawkins Communications Institute, which involved the study of dyadic communication and the use of API research procedures. In addition, I have worked closely and effectively with other research personnel. My writing ability and analytical skills have been developed through course work and practical experience.

Enclosed is my resume, which outlines my qualifications in further detail. I would welcome the opportunity to discuss my qualifications with you. I will phone within eight to ten days to see if an appointment can be arranged.

Very truly yours,

Sheila Farns

Enclosure

Cover Letter for Career Change

> John Hawkins
> 1815 H Street, NW
> Suite 1000
> Washington, DC 20006

> May 2, 1989

Mr. Greg Smethel
5100 M Street, NW
Washington, DC 20007

Dear Mr. Smethel:

Aside from being the largest oil producer and distributor in the United States, your company has an excellent reputation for offering one of the best management training programs in the country. Please consider my resume in response to your advertisement in The Washington Post.

After teaching high school social studies for seven years, I realize that I'm not using all of my abilities. Teaching is a wonderful profession in that you learn how to work closely with others on a day-to-day basis, but it didn't give me the chance to grow, express my ideas, and contribute to a large organization.

I need the challenge and excitement of working for a large organization such as yours. In addition to having the organizational and management skills necessary to be a productive corporate executive, I am success oriented and I would bring that characteristic to a management position.

Please consider me for the next training session, which begins in three weeks. I look forward to hearing from you, and to meeting you.

> Sincerely,
>
> John Hawkins

Enclosure

Chapter 6

DRACULA WILL SEE YOU NOW

There is a lot for you to learn in this chapter. When you have finished, you'll be able to do all the right things while you are sitting in front of an executive getting grilled. Obviously, practicing for the interview is a good idea, and knowing what kind of questions to look out for, you can think up some terrific answers ahead of time.

You still might get nervous and start twiddling your thumbs, or forget to look relaxed, or start mumbling, however. Sorry, but the only real practice for behaving well under pressure is to go through real interviews. For that reason, you should go get yourself interviewed as often as possible. It would be wise to run through a few interviews at your least interesting places before you go to the really important ones. If you networked and followed up on cold calls to track down jobs, you got a lot of practice as fast as possible.

There is something you can do at home to help yourself out, though. Fix your appearance and your attitude.

Appearance

Your dress should be in line with the company standards. If in doubt, wear a suit. Men and women. If you don't own a suit, now is a good time to invest in one. A few exceptions exist, but you are likely to know these. People interviewing as fashion designers, after all, should be fashionable.

> **To be yourself, start believing in yourself.**

Do not overdress. If everyone in the office wears fairly casual clothes, you won't feel too outrageous in a conservative suit. But watch the extra touches.

Take a look at yourself from head to foot. Do your heels need repair? Then repair them. Believe it or not, those little touches make a difference. The interviewer may not realize why you didn't look quite up to par, but she'll notice you didn't. Sew on all the buttons to your overcoat; this isn't the time to plan on leaving it in the waiting room quietly. Things might not work out that way.

If you have never been particular about your appearance, get advice from someone who knows how to dress professionally, or consult the following references:

The Professional Image by Susan Bixler (Putnam, 1984)

The Executive Look by Mortimer Levitt (AMACOM, 1979)

Image Impact for Men by Jacquline Thompson (Dodd, 1983)

Color Me Beautiful by Carole Jackson (Ballantine Books, 1984)

Executive Style: Looking It, Living It by Diana Lewis Jewell (New Century Pub., 1983)

The Appearance of Personality

Clothes are the easy part. You are part of your own appearance. Within minutes, an interviewer will have a preliminary opinion about you that is based completely on your looks. Not whether you are pretty or ugly, expensively or modestly dressed. More subtle things.

Watch someone you don't know for just 2 minutes. Now, honestly, don't you have some opinions about that person? The things people convey—accurately or not—by the way they conduct themselves include:

1. Maturity or immaturity

2. Conceit, confidence, or lack of confidence

3. Self-assurance or timidity

4. Cooperativeness or belligerence

Dressing for the First Impression

If an employer were to walk into a room and give one person a management-level job, he or she would naturally gravitate to someone who follows this dress code. It is corporate America's safe look. It bespeaks seriousness and career orientation.

WOMEN

Suit Wear a solid color. Do not wear a solid color jacket with a patterned skirt. Wearing a suit with a matching jacket and skirt makes a more powerful impact. Select a simple but elegant coordinating blouse. Choose an effective accent for a touch of personal flair; for example, a scarf or unique piece of jewelry.

Hemline 3 inches below knee to midcalf. Not to knee or above.

Stockings Silk finish. Same color or lighter than shoe.

Shoes 2-inch or 3-inch closed-toe pumps, little detail on shoes.

Purse Matches shoes. No oversized bags or evening clutches.

Jewelry No dangling bracelets or drop or hoop earrings. No more than two rings on hands.

Hair Professional style, clean, no ornaments on hair. Avoid hair below shoulders. Avoid "wet look" for hair.

Makeup Natural look, not heavy application. Lipstick and nail polish should be subtle colors and coordinated with suit.

Overall image If you can't afford to buy expensive clothes, buy clothes that look expensive. Avoid fabrics that wrinkle easily. Select items that look like real wool, cotton, or linen, or polyester that looks like silk—silk wrinkles!

MEN

Suits Dark gray and navy blue are the best colors to wear for an interview.

Shirts White or light blue cotton shirts are best. Cuffs should end below the wrist bone.

Ties Not too narrow or too wide. Select a tie with an evenly spaced small pattern or stripes. Do not wear flashy ties.

Hair Avoid long sideburns and beards. Keep hair out of your face. Have hair trimmed several days before interview.

Socks Select dark shades that match the color of your shoes or suit.

Shoes Select black or brown shoes. Coordinate shoes with suit. Avoid loafers, high heels, and buckles on shoes. Be sure to shine shoes before interview.

Is it drab and anonymous? No! It does deemphasize the costume to draw attention to the face—which is where your personality shines anyway. Women have lots of room within the code for individualization—a special pin or necklace and wonderful blouse can take you well beyond the navy-blue-suit-and-string-of-proper-pearls-cookie-cutter look. Men do have fewer options in colors and accessories, but they have another secret edge. Fit. As soon as possible, get a good suit tailor-fitted to you. Nothing will make you look more like an outsider than a collar gaping at the back or an orangutan-length sleeve.

5. Poise or edginess
6. Openness or evasiveness
7. Honesty or dishonesty
8. Intelligence or stupidity
9. Friendliness or hostility
10. And on, and on.

Besides what people sense in what you show them, they will automatically start to color their whole perception of you in ways that seem to fit together.

> **Women: Don't overdo jewelry or makeup.**

The interviewer will interpret your answers to fit the personality he or she invents for you.

If you seem honest and self-assured, the interviewer will probably interpret a pause in answering a question to be a sign of thoughtfulness. If the interviewer got the idea from your appearance and mannerisms that you were evasive, the same pause will be seen as a bad sign: maybe you are hiding something.

It's beside the point that this is a little unfair. It happens. So make things go well for yourself by presenting the best appearance possible. Be watchful of your grooming. Embarrassment about your scuffed shoes can make you avoid eye contact and make the employer judge you badly. Posture is also part of your appearance—an important one. Posture is discussed along with the other nonverbal clues.

Your best tactic is to seem to say in all your actions, "I'm interested. I believe in myself. I'm really paying attention."

How you do this breaks down into two parts: (1) adopting a wise attitude toward the interview process, and (2) minding your nonverbal manners.

Attitude

Attitude comes first, because it will carry you through when you forget your practiced answers and nonverbal manners. The most important thing to strive for is *honesty*.

Second most important: remember why you are sitting there getting a good look-over. Because you are begging for a job? Wrong. Begin to see the process from the other side.

Can you make this person's life better? Concentrate on answering *that* question during the interview while you also find out everything you want to know about the job and the company.

With varying choices by different firms, the most wanted characteristics of the ideal employee include these traits:

Will to achieve	Involvement
Will to succeed	Helpfulness
Desire for recognition	Adaptability

Drive
Pride
Willingness to compromise
Tolerance
Perseverance
Determination
Creativity
Independence
Flexibility

Open-mindedness
Empathy
Politeness
Adherence to traditional values
Strong belief in work ethic
Respect for authority
Leadership
Emotional stability

Do you have many of these attributes? Do they show easily? Let the employer see these good traits. In conversation, mention things you have done that show them. Go easy here. Just give the facts; don't brag.

The best advice (and the hardest to follow) is BE YOURSELF.

Look at that list. You have a lot to offer, don't you? The interviewer will never know about this good side unless you can relax and let it come out in your natural way. If you are the type that automatically answers, "Oh, not really," to all compliments, get rid of that habit. Immediately.

Even if you have to carry a list in your wallet, make yourself extremely aware of your own good traits. Tape them to your mirror. Keep a diary that includes one compliment to yourself every day.

> **Men: White or neutral is the best shirt color.**

A change in attitude does not come from thinking you ought to change. Knowing what to do is not good enough. You must change your attitude by force—by acting it out. Start with compliments. The next time you get one, just say, "Thank you," and shut up. Even if you blush furiously, feel queasy, want to say, "Oh, not really," with all your might. Just let it pass. The more you practice, the less it will torture you.

What Employers Don't Want

The person employers say they do not want is:
- Aggressive
- Critical
- Vindictive
- Restless
- Confrontational
- Antiestablishment
- Vocal
- Too happy-go-lucky
- Rebellious
- Bullheaded/hardheaded
- Uncertain

Employers also avoid hiring the person who apparently:
- Desires to be led
- Lacks tenacity
- Has a poor work history
- Has a poor family background—single, single parent, divorced
- Has financial and emotional problems

The last two items aren't even fair. What is more, using them as criteria for not hiring is illegal. Employers cannot ask what age you are or whether you are married, support children, have a spouse who drinks, or pay your bills on time or other such personal and non-job-related questions. "Have you ever been committed to the hospital for emotional problems?" is not permissible. Employers are on their own here—limited to noticing that someone seems too nervous to deal with the public, or doesn't seem to understand what the job requires.

You do not have to answer such questions. A very polite refusal on the grounds that it does not concern the job will suffice, or you could say that your career is your top priority. You must understand this is a real world, though. An employer whose last two single parents nearly ruined the company's reputation because they were always out sick has a real worry load. Your main reason for being here is what? To show you can reduce that employer's worry. You may choose to reveal personal information if you are comfortable doing so and you think it reduces the interviewer's reasonable worries. Just remember to use your good judgment here.

Shouts No One Hears

Nonverbal behavior can be more powerful than anything you say or put on your resume. The way you get your nonverbal good manners together is by maintaining a healthy attitude. Nonverbal moves and twitches speak about what you are feeling, not what you are consciously saying.

Nervous Behaviors

Nervousness is quite normal in an interview. You can easily control such obvious signs as picking invisible lint off your clothes, toe tapping, and sitting on the edge of your chair. A slip or two at the beginning will not necessarily ruin you—depending upon the job and the interviewer. The best thing you can do about this is go for lots of interviews, prepare for them very well, and think out the answers to some likely questions ahead of time.

The other thing you can do is remain aware of the nervous signals you are likely to give and replace them with nonnervous signs. When you discover that you are sitting rigidly on the edge of your chair, relax your muscles and sit back. Hold your hands more still, etc., until the normal conversational process puts you at ease.

Common Nervous Mannerisms

   Rigid posture
   Fiddling with hands
   Men—jiggling one leg rapidly
   Women—foot wiggling or toe tapping
   Excessive throat clearing
   General fidgeting—looking through papers, etc., instead of looking at person
   Smoking too much—no smoking is the best approach
   Smiling too much
   Nervous laughter

Eye-to-Eye Manners

Few people raised in this culture will fail to know how important it is to "look 'em in the eye." Good manners allow a break in eye contact as well. Too much direct looking makes people nervous.

Good eye contact means looking and looking away. When the interviewer points out a poster, look at the poster. A dead eyelock is not the thing at all. Move your head, shift from sharp attentive focus to a general focus. You do it all the time with friends and people that interest you. Let this person interest you.

One of the most effective nonverbal techniques is proper turn taking. On the verbal level you should answer questions and ask some of your own. Nonverbally, you should respond to the interviewer as well. When she talks, listen quietly. In pauses, nod your head, or utter "uh-huh" or some other common approval sound.

People do not accurately estimate how much of any conversation they monopolize. Effective turn-taking gestures will leave the impression that you contributed actively to the conversation. You may do as little as 5 percent of the talking. Most interviewers are not trained. As you begin to answer a question they might break in and go rambling along.

Turn taking creates a shared occasion. Appropriate gestures include:
- Inviting the other person to pass through the door first
- Handing any documents you bring with you to the interviewer instead of just showing them
- Leaning forward and showing that you would like to handle or get a better view of any pictures or documents the interviewer is handling
- Nodding where appropriate
- Repaying courtesies—simple things like passing back the sugar bowl when you see the other person needs it

These gestures establish a relationship between equals in an inoffensive way that would be very hard to do in words. In speech, you must balance between being too meek and being so forward that you seem pushy. Gestures are a natural meeting ground.

Posture

Most books will tell you not to slouch. It's decent advice, but a little off the mark. Slouchers get jobs, too. Good posture beats slouching, but slouching is not such a simple act. One person's slouch is offensively aggressive. Someone else's slouch is comfortably fine.

What you should be more aware of is your shoulder shape. Rounded shoulders are a major put-off. It makes people look lifeless, beaten, worn down, dull, plodding, uncreative. If you have a tendency to round your shoulders, do the following two posture exercises every day.

Posture Exercise 1. Several times a day imagine that a string is growing out of the very top of your head at the back. Someone tugs it gently upward. Your body follows until it feels just barely stretched in a pleasant way. While stretched notice your shoulders. Is there a tightness around the neck? Are your shoulders pointed forward with your chest sunken in? Lower your shoulders easily by imagining that someone is gently pulling down on your elbows. This is especially easy to feel if your arm is bent.

Women, particularly, tend to cross arms and hug themselves when they feel threatened. If you do this just sometimes, practice the exercises too. They will help you become more familiar with the right body feel to revert to when you catch yourself curling inward.

Posture Exercise 2. For this one, you'll be more comfortable at home or somewhere unobserved. It's not meant for elevators.

1. Stand with your feet about 6 inches apart.
2. Raise your arms (without any bend in the elbow) straight in front of you. The palms should be down, arms about level with shoulder. Hook thumbs.
3. Bend elbows to bring your hooked hands in to your chest.

4. Unhook thumbs and straighten your arms as you bring them behind your back. Don't turn your hands over; when you are halfway there, you should not look as if you are to be hung from a cross—your palms are facing behind you. Quite a feat. Now continue to bring your arms backward until you can hook your thumbs again behind your back. If you can't quite make it, bend your arms just enough to let you get your hands together.

5. Hold this position momentarily.

6. Now raise your arms (still hooked) upward to shoulder level.

7. Bend backward slightly while your arms are still up.

8. Hold this position to the count of 10.

9. Now bend forward and bring your hooked arms as high overhead as is comfortable.

10. Straighten slowly.

11. Let your arms fall to your side and relax.

The exercise is much simpler than the explanation sounds. Work through it. It is one of the most powerful techniques possible to teach you how your body should feel when it is properly stretched and relaxed. It's also great for tension. Do not force yourself or strain. Just go as far as is comfortable; eventually you will do this easily.

At Last, the Interview

All this and we haven't even talked about talking! You have been preparing for this for a long time. Already you have done several things that are going to enhance your performance.

1. You have pinned down what kind of person you are and what kind of job will fit you.

2. You really have a handle on what your skills are and what they can transfer to.

3. You have researched the company and know as much as possible about it.

4. You know what you don't know about the facility, the company, etc. These are the basis of your questions to the interviewer.

Research on the company is vital to doing a good job on the interview. Some employers estimate that only 5 percent of the applicants they see know anything about the company. They are impressed favorably with those who do know something. If you have an interview scheduled, ask the company for a copy of the annual report or latest newsletter before going. Look in those directories, too, for as much as you can learn.

The following information is of the type you will need in order to develop a company profile that will be useful to you in your interviews:

1. Expanding areas of the company

2. High turnover rates

3. Company mergers (often create new opportunities)

4. Company competitors

5. Most/least successful product/services the company offers

6. Problems the company is facing

7. Projected employment needs

8. Legislation that affects the company

9. Industry jargon

Your knowledge will help you make intelligent conversation. Employers look for people who can speak articulately. Answer questions in enough detail to satisfy the interviewer's interest, but don't overwhelm. You don't have to exhaust everything you know. Concise, clear, thoughtful answers are the ideal.

The employer is looking at you and wondering:

1. What you can do

2. What you want to do

3. Whether you fit in

4. How trainable you are and whether you can grow

The following resources and directories (most of which can be found in a public library) will be useful when you are developing your company profiles:

America's Corporate Families: The Billion Dollar Directory

Directory of Corporate Affiliations

The Dow Jones–Irwin Guide to Franchises

Engineering News-Record Directory of Contractors

Fortune Double 500

Fortune World Business Directory

International Directory of Corporate Affiliations

Investment Companies

Major Companies of Europe

Principal International Businesses

Standard and Poor's Register

Ward's Business Directory

Corporation Annual Reports of the Fortune 500

Interview Preparation Checklist

Before the actual interview:

- Review your skills, experience, and interests.
- Write your resume.
- Confirm interview date and time.
- Research the company.
- Gather references.
- Identify interviewer's name and title.
- Select appropriate attire.
- Prepare questions to ask the interviewer.
- Go through mock interview.

Another Round of Honesty

Once again we bring up honesty. You need not walk in and confess every shortcoming, but you do need to handle questions about your failures and put your skills in a realistic light.

Be honest without making too much of your negatives. The answer to "What's your worst trait?" should be something like "I work too hard" or "I set extremely high goals for myself."

More Good Things to Tell

You have already become familiar with one list of good traits that appeal to employers. Other things that employers look for include:

- Proven performance
- Good understanding of company goals
- Ability to advance
- Ability to work without excessive supervision
- Eagerness
- Friendliness
- Ease in giving and taking of the work load, duties, responsibilities
- Objectivity
- Maturity
- Willingness to take a risk
- Ability to handle stress well
- Predictability and reliability
- High self-motivation
- Drive and follow-through
- Analytical ability
- Problem-solving ability
- Good communications skills
- Well-groomed appearance
- Self-confidence
- Growth in the career so far
- Lack of personal problems, or the ability to handle them well
- Energy

You're an Interviewer, Too

It may not come until the very end, but you should always ask some questions during the interview. Usually the best starting question is not "How much can you pay me?"

2. How did you hear about us?

3. Why do you think you would like to work here?

4. What do you think it takes to be successful in a company like ours?

5. What do you expect to accomplish here?

6. How do you think you'll get along here?

7. What would you like to know about us?

8. What area of _____ fits you most?

After the Interview

Thank-Yous

Send thank-yous to everyone who has interviewed you. Do not neglect this. This is a business contact. Type your note in a standard business style. Include a mention of some point you discussed or highlight of the interview to remind the person which one of the many you were.

Assessment

After you complete each interview, you should take some time to assess how you did. Were there some moments when things did not go smoothly? Why? What could you improve on? What happened that you were not prepared for? What aspects of the interview went extremely well? You want to make sure that you carry those over to your next interview.

Rate your interview in the following categories so that you can learn from each interview and make the next one that much more successful.

Rating Scale
1—Excellent
2—Good
3—Fair
4—Poor/Needs improvement

Verbal

1. Expressed appropriate enthusiasm for position.

2. Focused on personal accomplishments, strengths, and skills.

3. Answered questions specifically, avoiding generalities.

4. Included relevant details in answers.

5. Did not interrupt interviewer.

6. Indicated knowledge of and interest in the field and organization.

7. Discussed how skills acquired through education or work are transferable to this position.

8. Used interviewer's name.

9. Expressed self with clear diction and good grammar.

10. Conveyed confidence.

11. Listened attentively.

12. Clarified decision-making time frame with employer before leaving.

13. Avoided criticism of former employers and coworkers.

14. Contributed important information about self.

15. Asked intelligent questions.

Nonverbal

1. Entrance and handshake were positive.

2. Dressed properly and professionally for interview.

3. Maintained eye contact with interviewer.

4. Gestures were relaxed, not stilted.

5. Voice projected enthusiasm.

6. Avoided distracting mannerisms.

7. Held appropriate posture (not too rigid or too round-shouldered).

8. Avoided using filler words, such as "you know," "okay," "right?" etc.

9. Spoke at a comfortable rate.

Follow-Up

1. Sent thank-you letter to interviewer.

2. Followed up on any requests made by interviewer during interview (sending examples of work, etc.)

Keep records while you're interviewing, including the following information:

1. Interview date_____

2. Company_____

3. Address_____

4. Type of firm_____

5. Interviewer's name_____

6. Phone number_____

7. Job title_____

8. Salary_____

9. Duties_____

10. Call the interviewer by_____

11. Interviewer will call me by_____

12. Information I need to send interviewer_____

13. Thank-you note sent_____

14. Additional comments_____

_____

Chapter 7

BUT OUR PRESIDENT DOESN'T MAKE THAT MUCH!

It happened. The call or letter finally came offering you a job. Do you want it? Whether you get one offer or several, the process is the same. You want to know:

1. Is this my kind of place?
2. Can I continue to grow in this company?
3. Is my future boss someone I can work with?
4. Is the pay acceptable?
5. Are the benefits adequate?

When you get your offer, slow down. Don't rush into saying yes unless you are very sure it's right for you.

My Kind of Place

You should already know whether the company seems right. Go to your interview notes. What was your reaction and why? Be mature here. When you began your job hunt, you may have had unreasonable expectations. Later on you may have reacted more favorably to a similar situation at another company as you learned what to expect.

You should have asked questions about employee turnover, the chance for responsibility, management style, and other things that lead to making a smart move.

Will Growing Be a Pain?

We hope you asked. What the company offers down the road can matter much more than what it is offering you right now.

If growth is limited, you have another decision to make. You must decide whether the company is offering you a good introduction to the field. Or valuable training. Or adequate prestige for later on.

You also need to ask yourself if you really want to begin this job hunt business again very soon.

If you need advanced skills or education to grow in the company, what are your chances of getting it? Will the company pick up the tab? Can you (and will you) get it on your own?

Bosses, Buddies, and Bullies

You could get through school with one rotten teacher among the good. That may not work in the big world. Your direct supervisor can help you a lot. Can ruin you too.

If you didn't talk to the person who would be your immediate supervisor during your interview, ask to meet him or her now. This is a reasonable request if the company is local. Consider footing the bill to travel to an out-of-town site. Often companies will pay your fare, or part of it anyway.

Remember the earmarks of a good mentor:

1. A good self-opinion, but not a big ego

2. Compatible viewpoint and energy level

3. Technical expertise and political savvy

4. Enthusiasm for his or her job and a strong desire to share it with someone promising

You would benefit from talking to people who are working for, or have worked for, your potential boss. Find out if he or she gave them a helping hand and encouragement.

Some mentor types are deprived. They would love to pull someone along but just haven't found anyone willing. This can be a big problem in government offices. Employees land in their jobs with a thud, expecting raises by formula and high security despite performance but offering little beyond their bare duties to their office. In such places a mentor can be aching to find just one eager person. But watch out, still. Some places are so hidebound, your mentor may not be able to help you past the million and one personnel rules and regulations that set your promotional pace. Stay away from offices that are propelled by nitwits just putting in time and martyrs who are doing great work without adequate recognition.

A mentor can do much for you:

- Sponsor your job opportunities and advancement
- Make fences fall, pulling you into responsible positions faster than normal
- Guide you by his or her acquired wisdom
- Make you known to people who count
- Send the most interesting, challenging, and satisfying work your way
- Help you get training or pertinent conference opportunities
- Give you room to run risks but protect you from real blunders
- Leave you alone to work in your own style

Usually, a mentor is also a friend.

Just what makes a bad boss? Not always personality. Some terrific people are horrible bosses. Think long and hard before hooking up with bosses that:

- Give such exacting directions that you turn into a good (but mindless) robot
- Give no guidance at all, leaving you in the dark about what you should achieve, what the goals are, when work is due, how much is needed, etc.
- Don't tell you when you are off the track but just give the work to someone else and quit believing in you
- Steal your work, or ideas, and the credit you should get
- Show jealousy of others who have ideas and ambition, or threaten them
- Maintain too much distance
- Promise but don't follow through
- Cannot set priorities, change direction frequently, and keep running on a crisis schedule at all times

What Is Your Fair Market Value?

The less experience you have, the less you know about the fair value of your employment. You have an offer now. It's time you found out what's fair.

All sorts of charts, lists, and tables exist of average wages by profession. Use these as a guide, but remember that "average" implies that some are lower and some are higher.

The reasons you might get a low offer include:

1. They're just kidding a little; they expect you to haggle for more.

2. They're genuine cheapskates.

3. The company is too new, too small, or too poor to go any higher right now.

4. The market is crowded and, no matter what the tables say, you're lucky to get this.

5. This locale pays lower than national averages or other cities.
6. Your experience, skills, or training is somewhat lower than average, but they'll bet on you.
7. You're really in the range—the average includes a very wide spread.
8. This industry pays less for this work than an equivalent job would bring in another industry.
9. This is not a priority function; the company is investing more in other critical skill areas.
10. The benefits package is better.

To get an idea of fair pay, you can go to several sources. One of the easiest to compare is the federal wage. Go to the nearest federal personnel office. Look up your job description and criteria for filling it. See what rate (grade level) it is given. This will tell you what the range is. Entry-level (Step 1) comparisons are most compatible because the government will give regular raises just for showing up day after day. A similar performance in industry could cost your job. Hardly anyone loses a government job as a direct result of poor performance. It isn't worth the hassle to the boss, who doesn't have to turn a profit anyway.

> **When you get your offer, slow down.**

Other sources are *The Almanac of American Employers* in a public library, and *Monthly Labor Review*. College placement offices often have local and national information on file.

You can also scout the territory. It is possible to go back through your network again. Talk to people who didn't hire you to find out what they pay.

The Department of Labor keeps records too. You can get a copy of minimum rates by wage class and by locality for the many jobs that are rated.

Rating Your Offer

Money in your pocket now is the first thing you should check in rating a job offer. Evaluate your offer systematically. Use the following chart to be sure you count the same things at each possible place.

Gross monthly salary $_____

Health benefits	Your contribution	+ employer's contribution	+/– _____
Retirement	Your contribution	+ employer's contribution	+/– _____
Car used in the job	Your costs (include a portion of insurance and maintenance)	+ worth of use of a company car / it saves you from buying another car	+/– _____

(continued)

Transportation	Fares		+/− _____
	Monthly parking and tips		+/− _____
Phone	Long-distance calls to office on your own money		+/− _____
Stock options	Your contribution	+ (future gain / count lightly, this is not dependable income)	+/− _____
Income reduction plans in nonprofit organization	What do you choose to withhold	+ tax savings	+/− _____
Lunches, etc.	Allowance you'll need to get by in this setting	+ lunches provided by expense account / count only the rate of your normal daily cost, despite the fact you may eat better on an expense account	+/− _____
Child care	Cost based on hours needed (including commuting time)	+ employer's contribution or benefits	+/− _____
Perquisites		+ value of tickets, health club or other / count only what you'd probably spend anyway	+/− _____
Net take-home pay			+/− _____

We Also Have Health, Life, and Balloon Rides on the Fourth of July

Benefit packages vary in surprising ways. The surprise could be bad if you don't analyze them carefully. Say two jobs both pay $1,200 a month and both employers have life insurance, health insurance, ten days of sick leave, etc. Your take-home pay, though, might be $750 at one place and $890 at the other. Why? One employer pays 80 percent of your insurance; the other offers a more grand (and expensive) package, but you pay for it.

Look at each benefit carefully. A bonus based on net profit at year end isn't good if the company accountants are clever at calling surplus income anything but profit. If a bonus is offered, make sure the company has really paid these in the past.

Sick leave is a courtesy. Good employers allow for it. Good employees do not use it for a vacation. If sick leave abuse doesn't cost you your job, it can certainly retard your promotion. If it's vacation you want, go to the company that offers vacation or flexible schedules.

Profit sharing is a very forward-looking benefit. Companies that offer this usually view employees as the source of success. Not only can it mean extra money for you, it can mean that you found a company that likes its people.

Executive benefit packages can be so rewarding that they are called "golden handcuffs." Even below the executive level, watch out for benefit handcuffs. You don't want to work at a poorly chosen place just because the benefits are so good.

The other common mistake about benefits is to overrate the "bird in the bush." You need money. The amount in pocket today is what you live on—no matter how fantastic the options, bonuses, or retirement plans may be.

Counting Your Chickens—Evaluating Retirement Plans

Forecasters expect we will change jobs much more often in the future than our parents did. This throws retirement under a new light. Some industries are especially volatile; moving around is standard. A retirement plan you become vested in after ten years is no good to the employee who leaves in eight.

If retirement is an important benefit to you, check the vesting schedule. Once you are fully vested, you will draw according to what you and your employers put in. Some plans offer an increasing percentage of vesting as the years go by, meaning you will draw something. If not vested, you may recover your contribution to the plan but not the portion paid by your employer.

Once you are vested, the company cannot cancel your rights. You are now protected by federal legislation.

If you expect to move on, extra cash in hand to invest in your private plan can be better than a good company plan you'll never collect.

Job Rating System

Evaluate these factors for each job on a scale from 1 to 10.

1. How much do you like this place?___
2. How good is the management?___
3. How promising is your potential boss?___
4. Opportunity for growth.___
5. Job security.___
6. Chance for challenging work.___
7. Chance to control your own work.___
8. Management opportunity.___
9. Training opportunity.___

Put an asterisk (*) by the factors you discovered were most important to you.

Now write down:

10. Net take-home pay. $___
11. Benefits:___

What to Do If You Want Another Job

You want very much to work at one place, but another company offers you a job first. What do you do now?

1. Ask the company that made the offer for some time to think it over.
2. Call the other company. Explain you have an offer but would like to work with them. Ask for a decision before your deadline to respond to the first company.
3. Be sure that an offer from the second company is valid before turning down the first offer.

What If the Offer Is Too Low?

First, make a counteroffer. Be prepared to justify your work. Your outstanding bills are not as compelling as your outstanding talents, though.

Your second line of defense if you want the job anyway is to negotiate an early review. Accept the salary for six months, for instance, with a predetermined raise at the end if your performance is satisfactory. Employers take a risk with each new employee. If you believe in yourself, you may well sell this idea. Once you're proven, the fear of throwing good money on a bad bet will be over.

Caution: if you don't get this in writing, be sure to include the agreement in your letter of acceptance. Get it on paper for your own protection.

Acceptance

Always accept jobs in writing. Restate any agreements you made about starting dates, salary, review periods, and so on.

Now you have the complete course. If you skimmed to here, go back and get to work. If you read along without doing the exercises, making the phone calls, or trying any of the hard parts, we wish you luck. You must be counting on it.

The Job Hunter's Workbook follows a philosophy you've heard before: "To thine own self be true." We can give you no better advice. The career you've always dreamed of is possible only for those who know themselves. Every step in this book is based on that guiding philosophy.

Your work in getting to know what you are like, what pleases you or annoys you, what you want, what you can offer, and where you can find the right job is the hard ground of building a successful career. Be careful, perseverant, and honest in these parts, and your career will be just what you want. We wish you luck also, but you won't need it. You'll make your own.